Washington Gladden

The Cosmopolis City Club

Washington Gladden

The Cosmopolis City Club

ISBN/EAN: 9783743308572

Manufactured in Europe, USA, Canada, Australia, Japa

Cover: Foto ©ninafisch / pixelio.de

Manufactured and distributed by brebook publishing software
(www.brebook.com)

Washington Gladden

The Cosmopolis City Club

THE
COSMOPOLIS CITY CLUB

BY

Rev. WASHINGTON GLADDEN

NEW YORK
THE CENTURY CO.
1893

CONTENTS

CHAPTER I

PAGE

How the Club was Organized 7

CHAPTER II

The Club Gets to Work 51

CHAPTER III

What the Club Accomplished 90

PREFACE

THE publication in the "Century Magazine," of the following narrative brought me a great many interesting letters from all parts of the country. In several cities, as it appeared from this correspondence, movements not unlike the one here imagined were already in progress. From one of the cities of the Empire State came the report which follows:

In 1890 a small number of the citizens of this city formed a Law and Order Alliance, having for its object the idea expressed in the Cosmopolis City Club; but unfortunately there was no one who could outline a practical plan for accomplishing any good work. There were several members who advocated radical measures, similar to those entertained by Mr. Frambes, but others counseled moderation, deprecating the policy of taking upon themselves the duties of detectives and policemen, and yet unable to suggest any other practical method. The society has drifted along with a small membership, keeping up its organization, and making now and then a spasmodic attempt to influence, if possible, the city officials to a proper fulfilment of their duties. In July of 1892 I was elected Secretary of the Alliance, and since then I have been struggling to find the right way to go about the work we need to do. I sincerely believe you have given us the right clue.

From one of the chief cities of Pennsylvania came another testimony dated January 10, 1893. It is written by Mr. Robert B. Lea, the secretary of the association described:

The line of thought and the plan suggested in your article, "The Cosmopolis City Club" published in the "Century" of January, 1893, is so much in accord with the objects and work of our Citizens' Reform Association, that I feel constrained to write you and say that, coming at this particular time, your article was not only encouraging, but was an exceedingly good campaign document for us. Our city primary elections were held on January 7, and this association was greatly interested therein, because one of its originators was the Reform candidate for Mayor, and because we had Reform candidates for City Councils throughout the city. As the "Century Magazine" is read, to a great extent, by the people who do not, as a rule, turn out at the primaries, and as many of these called my attention to the article, I think I am warranted in saying that it

had considerable influence with this class of our
citizens.

Perhaps a brief history of our association
may prove interesting to you. For some time
past the city government of Allegheny has been
an exceedingly corrupt one. This state of affairs
led several gentlemen to hold a meeting, about
a year ago, at the residence of one of their members, to talk the situation over, and see if something could not be done to stop the loose and
dishonest methods then in force. To show how
like to our plan is the one suggested by your
article, at that meeting were a physician, a bank
president, three attorneys, a merchant, a manufacturer, an insurance agent, and a bookkeeper.
After considerable discussion, a temporary organization was effected, which resulted finally in "The
Citizens' Reform Association of Allegheny, Pennsylvania," an organization now strong in numbers,
and composed of all classes of citizens. The first
important work of this association was the intro-
duction into the City Councils of an ordinance calling for the appointment of an auditing committee,
and instructing this committee to audit all the city
books. After hard work, and with the assistance
of councilmen favorable to reform, the measure
was finally passed, and a very good auditing committee appointed. Without going into details,
the work of this committee resulted in the arrest,
conviction, and imprisonment of the City Market
Clerk and the Mayor of the city, in a general

purging of the city offices, and, last but not least, in the nomination and election of the present Reform Mayor, whom we have just renominated for another term.

Many other reform measures have been put in force by this Association, but this was one of the most important. To-night is our first annual election, so you see we are still young. The organization is permanent, and will in the future look closely after city affairs.

Another similarity between your plan and ours is the assignment of the different city departments to special committees. Our executive committee, as you will notice from the by-laws inclosed, is composed of nine members, and a certain department of the city government is allotted to each. This work, although very important, has not been followed up as it should have been, but will be in the future, since a knowledge of these departments is absolutely necessary in order to work intelligently and successfully.

These reform movements are always looked upon as the work of soreheads, or the attempt of one set of men to oust another, so as to get into place and power themselves. But this prejudice can be overcome, and after the confidence of the public has been gained, there is but little difficulty in making the work tell, and in getting the help and sympathy of all good citizens.

The appearance of your article at this time, with a plan so similar to ours, I regard as a striking coincidence. I have no doubt some will say of it "that is very good in theory, but will it work in practice?" Just refer any such to us for a practical demonstration of its feasibility.

An ounce of experience is worth a pound of theory, and Mr. Lea's interesting letter will justly carry more weight with many readers than the imaginary transactions of the Cosmopolis Club. It ought to be said, however, that these transactions are not all imaginary. Citizens of Philadelphia have not failed to recognize in certain reports presented to the Cosmopolis Club by its committees the results of investigations made by their own Municipal League, and quite a number of other passages will have a familiar sound to the residents of other cities.

The responses which have been made to my little story, not only through private letters, but also through the press, indicate a great awakening of public interest in this subject. The City Club of New York, with its permanent organization, and its plan of campaign that looks forward to years of persistent agitation, and to the establishment in every part of the city of popular Good Government Clubs, affiliated with itself, is the harbinger, I trust, of a vigorous movement on

the part of decent and law-abiding people in all
the cities of the land to secure better municipal
administration.

This little book does not exhaust the subject.
There is a great deal more to say. Many interesting phases of this important question are not
touched upon in these discussions. One suggestion in particular, recently made by Mr. Charles
Francis Adams, looking toward the abolition of
the ward as a political division, and the election
of councilmen on a general ticket, is worthy of
careful consideration. This change would require,
of course, a reform in the methods of voting, and
the adoption of some scheme of proportionate or
minority representation. But it is undoubtedly
true that the Council is generally the weak point
in the municipal government; and that the improved methods introduced into the executive departments of some of our cities have accomplished
less than they would have done if it had not been
for the inefficiency and the corruption of the municipal legislature. That the poor quality of municipal councils is due to an excess of localism
Mr. Adams has made plain; and the attention of
all students of city politics should be directed to
this phase of the question.

All that I have tried to do in the discussions
that follow is to present in a simple and concrete
form a few suggestions as to the methods in which
citizens may coöperate in the study of this subject, and a few hints as to the direction which
municipal reforms are likely to take. Nobody
can be more fully aware than I am that the conclusions here reached are not finalities. In the
political methods of a progressive people there
are no finalities. But I hope that this small book
may help to stir up the pure minds of a great
many good citizens to think soberly and patiently
upon the most important practical question now
before the American people.

COLUMBUS, O., April 25, 1893.   W. G.

THE COSMOPOLIS CITY CLUB

CHAPTER I

HOW THE CLUB WAS ORGANIZED

I

"NO, it is useless to talk; we shall get nothing out of that council this year. We are not the kind of people whom they delight to honor. If the library were only a gin-mill or a poker-den, its petition would be heard; the effectual fervent prayer of that sort availeth much at the city hall. But there are no ears for our supplications."

The speaker is resting his hand upon the mantelpiece, and warming his sturdy figure in the rays of a soft-coal fire. A stout, square-built young fellow, with a broad brow crowned by a shock of stiff hair brushed *à la pompadour*, and lighted with keen gray eyes; a born fighter, you would say, if you glanced at his firm jaw and well-shut lips. He is evidently the latest arrival of a group of five, the other members of which are gathered about the fireplace. The room is plainly

7

furnished with a large office-table in the center, and a few leather-covered chairs; maps and charts are the only decorations of the walls; a head of Homer and a bust of Sophocles look down from the solitary bookcase. It is the directors' room of the Cosmopolis Public Library, and the officials to whom it belongs are now in occupation.

The gentleman who has expressed opinions so dubious respecting the people at the city hall is Mr. Reginald Payne, lawyer. He has been commissioned by his colleagues to find out what might be the prospects of an increased appropriation for the purposes of the library, and this is his report. When it is delivered, he turns from the fire, pulls a chair into the circle, seats himself therein with some emphasis, and brings his two fists unequivocally down upon the arms thereof.

"To spend an hour and a half in that black hole," he continues, "makes a man feel like homicide."

"For a man who spends his days in courthouses, your disgust is somewhat surprising," laughs one of his auditors.

"Court-houses!" explodes the lawyer. "Why, parson, the court-house is a sanctuary compared with that council-chamber. The court-house is not, to be sure, the sweetest place in the world. All sorts of foul and crooked things are gathered into it, but they are there to be cleansed and rectified. That, on the whole, is what is going on in the court-house. The methods, indeed, are not always above criticism, and there are miscarriages of justice; but the net result of it all is righteousness. But your council-chamber — bah! It smells to heaven. Bad tobacco, stale beer, and the incense which always arises from assemblies of the great unwashed perfume the air, and the moral atmosphere is not less tainted."

"You are growing fastidious, Payne," laughs the other. "You must n't look for the representatives of culture in the municipal councils."

"Why not? Those are the people you look for and find in the city council of Berlin, of Glasgow, of Manchester, of Birmingham, of London; why should we not expect to see them in the governing bodies of our own cities?"

"Because," answers another of the group, "if you do, you 'll be awfully disappointed."

"Get thee behind me, pessimist!" cries the sturdy advocate. "I tell you what it is, John Tomlinson, this thing has got to stop. Yes, sir! That infernal hour and a half over in the council-chamber has burned some lessons into my soul. We must take hold of that place, and clean it out."

"The voice is the voice of Hercules," laughs the parson, "but the hands are the hands of Reginald Payne. I judge that this job will task their strength."

"It will take more than one pair, doubtless," rejoins the lawyer, springing to his feet. "It will call for the soiling of some that like to keep themselves white, like yours, Parson Morison; it will

need the coöperation of those sleek saints of yours
who so cheerfully describe themselves every Sunday as miserable sinners; it will need to enlist the
money of this town, Tomlinson; and its brains,
Harper; and its muscle, Hathaway," with a shoul-
der-hitting gesture in the direction of each of
these gentlemen: "but the thing can be done, and
it may as well start here as anywhere."

"But you have n't given us much information
yet," ventures Tomlinson. "We send you off on
a reconnaissance, and you come back and proceed
to storm our works. Cool off, young man, and
tell us what you have found out."

"Quite right," replies the lawyer; "it will not
take long. I found out, as I said, that you will
get no money from the council for the library.
'Millions for boodle, but not one cent for books,'
is the motto of these statesmen."

"Whom did you see?" asks Tomlinson.

"First I saw O'Halloran, the president. He
was talking with a base-ball delegation, and of
course he could not spare me much of his valua-
ble time; he said that our memorial was in the
hands of Herr Schwab, of the Ways and Means
Committee. I asked him what he thought of
the probability of its being favorably acted on.
He answered that the case was doubtful; the ap-
propriations were so large already that it was not
thought best to increase them. He advised me
to see Schwab. This magnate sat in his com-
mittee-room, wreathed in smoke and clothed upon

with majesty. A small group surrounded his desk: Smiley, the street contractor; Burns, his lawyer; and Mikey Flynn, the small boss of the Nineteenth Ward. From what I overheard, I knew that they were putting up a job to pave that street newly opened through the cow-pasture over on Worthington Heights. At length they withdrew, and I ventured into the august presence. The great man scarcely deigned to notice me at first. When I pressed my business upon his attention, he said, 'Oh, yas; die libarry; das you call de pook pildin' oop on Fon Buren sdreet, not so?' I admitted the accusation, and he went on: 'So you wandt vife tousand tollars of de beople's money for pooks, not so? I shall see, but I bromise not mooch. Die abbrobriations already is sehr heffy. Chim Mulloy he must haf his margot-house at the Nord Ent, and dat gost two hundert tousand tollar; and Gurnel Schneider he must haf his armory ofer de reefer, and dat gost ein hundert tousand more; and dar's shoost biles of sdreet imbrovements dis year—shoost biles of 'em. And I don'd see where any money's gomin' from to puy pooks.'

"I asked our chancellor of the exchequer if he intended to report favorably on our appropriation, but he was persistently non-committal. It was quite useless to waste words upon him, so I sought the other members of the committee, most of whom were in the council-chamber, and tried to interest them. They listened as patiently as they could, and agreed that the library was doing good work, and ought to be encouraged; but I saw in their eyes that they did not intend to give us anything. Some of them would, no doubt, if there had been any hint of a 'divvy,' but they are gentlemen who agree with the devil in the opinion that it is a stupid thing to serve God for naught; others who would gladly enough have given us what we ask are so frightened by the enormous extravagance into which the council has been rushing that they dare not add another dollar. The conclusion of the whole matter is that our memorial has n't the ghost of a chance to pass the council; we must get on as best we can without aid from the city."

"It is rather depressing," answers the gentleman addressed as Harper, after a few moments' silence. "The men who erected this building, and gave this library its liberal endowment, and made it free to the city, expected, and had a right to expect, that the city would replenish its shelves from year to year. We have income enough to pay the other expenses, but not enough to buy books; a few thousand dollars a year for books would vastly extend its usefulness. We are learning to use the library in our high-school work more and more; the librarian and the teachers are coöperating very intelligently. We are getting the pupils not only to read good books, but also — which is a thing hardly less important — we are teaching them to use books for purposes of refer-

ence,— to find things in books,— to know where
to look for the facts which they desire to know.
In order that this kind of work may be done in
the most serviceable way, the library must be constantly enlarged; not only must we have all the
newest and best reference books, but all the new
histories, manuals of literature, works upon political and social science, and so forth. The library,
properly stocked and properly used, is worth more
to the city for educational purposes than the five
best teachers in our schools ; and it is a melancholy fact that while Jim Mulloy can get two hundred thousand dollars for a market-house out in
that suburb, and Colonel Schneider can get a hundred thousand dollars for his armory, the library
should beg in vain at the door of our council for
a paltry gift of five thousand dollars."

"Melancholy indeed," answers Tomlinson; "but
you know very well that Jim Mulloy and Colonel Schneider sustain very different relations to
this council from those which you and I sustain. Several of these men were made councilors
by them, and must not the potter have power over
the work of his own hands? Besides, there is a
big real-estate job behind each of these enter-
prises, and convincing reasons could be shown to
many of these gentlemen why the erection of these
new buildings could not be deferred for an hour."

"Quite so," rejoins the lawyer. "And I have
been ruminating, while the principal here was
talking about the uses of the library, upon the

impression which his admirable exposition would
make upon the minds of those men down there,
if they could hear it. How much do you suppose
you could make them understand of the educational value of a public library?"

"Not much, alas!" replies the schoolmaster.
"And that is the melancholy fact. Why must a
fair, prosperous, respectable city like this be governed by men who have no comprehension of its
true interests, and no sense of the importance of
good government? Take the whole administration, from top to bottom, and apply to it the
ordinary business test. Is there a man in any of
the executive departments whom you, Tomlinson,
would trust as the manager of your factory?"

"Not one," answers the manufacturer.

"In the council," continues Harper, "there are
a few fairly good men, but they are either too
busy to give much careful attention to the affairs
of the city, or else too fastidious to grapple with
the corrupt elements of the council, and the result
is that the men who have gone into city politics
for what there is in it have things pretty much
their own way. Between inertia and inefficiency
on the one hand, and rascality on the other, the
business of our city is horribly mismanaged. Talk
about representative government! Does this governmental inaction down at the city hall represent
the people of Cosmopolis?"

"Yes," answers the clergyman, deliberately; "I
rather think it does."

"Do you mean to assert," persists the school-master, "that O'Halloran and his crew in the council-chamber, and the heads of the executive departments, are fair exponents of the intelligence and morality of this city?"

"Well, perhaps not of what may be described as the latent intelligence and conscience of the community. We may admit that there is a great deal of moral energy packed up and stored away in the minds and hearts of our citizens which is wholly inoperative. Its possessors are doing with it precisely what the man in the parable did with his one talent. This latent wisdom and virtue don't count. For all practical purposes they are non-existent. Of course they are not represented in the character of our city government. Why should they be? But our government fairly represents and expresses the *active* intelligence and conscience of the community. *Potential* morality must be ruled out in all practical estimates of political forces. All the wisdom and all the virtue of the community which are actually in motion have found representation in the city hall. The doctrine of causation does not fail us here. We are reaping exactly what we have sown."

"I suppose so," replies the other. "And what is the remedy for this state of things?"

"I should like to tell you, gentlemen, how the matter looks to me, if it was n't past my bedtime," says the one member of the group who has hitherto listened intently but silently. He is a mus-

cular man of medium height, with angular features
and bright eyes, and the hand with which he but-
tons his plain tweed coat bears the signature of
severe toil. The eyes of all the group are turned
toward him with evident sympathy and respect as
he rises to his feet. " I have been thinking pretty
hard," he goes on, " while you have been talking,
and some things seem very plain to me."

" Let us hear," says the clergyman.

" No; it is too late. You know that we working-men must be up in the morning."

" Let us meet here again one week from to-
night," proposes the manufacturer. " We have
raised a great question, and we must not drop it
here. I want to hear what Hathaway has been
thinking, for he always thinks to some purpose.
Possibly a week's reflection will clear all our
heads."

II

" WE are all here now, and Sam Hathaway has
the floor," is the cheery word of Reginald Payne,
as the five directors assembled in their sanctum on
the next Thursday evening.

" What I wanted to say last week," says the
carpenter, speaking slowly but directly, " has been
on my mind ever since, and it is as clear to me
now as it was then that we must have organization,
the organization of the industrious and respectable people of this city, to secure good government.

You may say that we have two organizations for
this purpose already — the Republican and the
Democratic party organizations. I don't wish to
use any hard words about these two political machines, but it is clear that they are not intended
to do the kind of work that we want done here.
Whatever Republicanism or Democracy may stand
for, it does n't stand for good municipal government. These parties are organized for other purposes; they have no interest in local affairs beyond
carrying elections and dividing spoils. When the
Republican party puts a presidential or a con-
gressional candidate into the field, he is supposed
to represent certain principles or policies which
can be discussed and commended to the people;
when the Republican party puts a candidate for
mayor or councilman into the field, he represents
nothing at all except the wish of the managers to
get possession of the offices. And it is precisely
so with the other party. Municipal contests under these party banners are therefore destitute of
meaning. There are no principles on either side
that can be defined or advocated; it is an unprin-
cipled scramble for spoils, that 's all. Now it
does n't need to be argued that such a method of
managing municipal politics will never give us
efficient government. It 's just like taking the
officers and clerks of a bank, and setting them to
work, once a year, to run a laundry. It 's just as
if you, Mr. Tomlinson, should try to transform
your big establishment for the manufacture of

2

harvesters into a watch-factory for one month of every year. It is not less absurd to expect that a big party organization which was made to do one kind of work will do equally as well another and a wholly different kind of work. When the national parties enter the municipal field, they leave all their principles behind them. And a party without principles — a party whose only reason for existence is the spoils — is always an unclean thing, and must pollute everything that it touches. This is, in my judgment, one main reason of the corruption of our municipal politics the country over. We have no organizations for municipal politics that have any relation whatever to municipal affairs. Therefore we have no intelligent or well-considered action upon municipal affairs. We must find some way of bringing our people together upon a platform broad enough to include all well-disposed citizens, and train them to coöperate for the promotion of good government in the city."

"Right you are!" cries Reginald Payne. "It takes a carpenter to hit a nail on the head. You've said exactly what I meant to say, but I forgive you. Give me your hand, Sam Hathaway!"

"Well, gentlemen," says the carpenter, blushing a little, as he grasps the hand of the impulsive lawyer, "there is one lesson that we working-men have learned, and that's the value of organization. You can't do much in these days without it. You've got to stand together if you want to ac-

complish anything. There must be a great many
people in this city, of all classes, who want good,
clean, efficient government. If we can get them
all, or even a good share of them, to stand together for this one thing, we can secure it."

"'If,'" says the sententious Tomlinson.

"Yes, 'if,'" echoes the exuberant lawyer. "The
trouble is to get the rank and file to break away
from their parties. It will take no little work to
overcome the idolatry of party. It can't be done
in one year, nor in half a dozen. It means a long,
persistent campaign of agitation and education.
And this work cannot begin too soon."

"You are right," says the manufacturer. "I do
not wish to be considered as a skeptic or a dissen-
ter. I cordially agree with all that Mr. Hathaway has said. As he was talking, I was reflecting
upon the fact that while the average voter in our
city is pretty well informed upon national issues,
he knows very little about municipal questions.
Most of our voters know something — enough to
have some sort of opinion — about the tariff, and
the silver question, and the Southern question;
how many of them have any, even the remotest,
conception of the methods of municipal organization? How many of them could tell you how this
city is governed? how its executive force is constituted? how its finances are managed? I'll venture that if you go down Jefferson street to-morrow,
and put these questions to the heads of all the
business houses, you will not get an intelligent

answer from one man in twenty. All this confirms what Hathaway has said, that our municipal politics are utterly devoid of educational value. There is no organization whose business it is to bring before the people the serious problems which all the while arise respecting the management of city affairs. We ought to have such an organization, and I agree with Payne that it cannot get to work too soon."

" We ought to have it," echoes the schoolmaster; " but how to get it — there is the rub. Who will set the thing in motion? Who will undertake to see that the child is reputably born and baptized?"

"And who," continues the lawyer, " will sit up nights with it till it gets its eye-teeth cut, and nurse it safely through the mumps and the measles? Infants of this sort require a great deal of mothering."

"No doubt of it," rejoins the manufacturer; "and somebody must make up his mind to lose considerable sleep, and to take upon himself no little care, if this thing is to live and grow. But is n't it worth a little labor and sacrifice to rescue our city from its present disgrace, and to put it into clean and competent hands? And is there any reason why we should not start this thing in motion?"

"But how?" persists the lawyer. "Shall we publish in the newspapers a call for a meeting?"

"No, no!" cries the schoolmaster. "Take any shape but that! Don't you know who will come?

Half the cranks in town, and none of the people whom you want to secure. The intelligent citizen is shy of the aggregations drawn together by such a summons."

"Let me make a suggestion," ventures the parson. "Let us see if we cannot work out this sum by Mr. Hale's rule of ten-times-one-are-ten. We are a fairly representative little group — business man, lawyer, educator, mechanic, minister. Suppose we appoint a meeting two weeks from to-night, and each of us agree to bring with him, if he can, ten of his associates — men with whom he is most intimately connected. Let Tomlinson have free range of the manufacturers, the merchants, and the bankers; let Payne loose among the lawyers and the judges; let Harper bring in teachers and editors — we want to have one or two of them; let Hathaway pick out some of the brightest and most sensible of the working-men; and I will invite — ten clergymen? No; I think that that would be a disproportionate number. But I will ask two or three of the other ministers, and two or three doctors, and a few other reputable persons whom I know. If each of us will use his best judgment in selecting men who are likely to be in sympathy with our project, I think that we may bring together a company of gentlemen who will give to our organization, at the outset, dignity and influence with all classes."

"Admirable!" cries the schoolmaster, and the whole company repeats the verdict.

" And yet," ventures Mr. Payne, " I think that
this scheme will bear amendment. Would n't it
be well to canvass these names here, before we
issue our invitations? I, for example, might, in
perfect good faith, select some man whom some
of you, knowing him a little better than I do,
would know to be an undesirable associate. Let
each man make out his list now, and submit it
for criticism."

This suggestion is readily adopted, and the next
hour is spent in preparing the lists and subjecting
them to careful scrutiny, with the result of elimi-
nating several doubtful names, and substituting
for them others whose merit is unquestionable.

" Now where shall we meet?" demands the
schoolmaster, when the final list has been com-
pleted.

" You might come to our chapel," says the rector,
dubiously, " but — "

" I would like to emphasize that ' but,' " breaks
in the manufacturer. " I know what Mr. Morison
means. It is n't wise to let this movement be
very closely identified with any form of ecclesias-
ticism. It ought to be in the largest sense of the
word catholic, comprehending all classes, all sects,
and all parties; and it must avoid everything that
could cast suspicion upon its catholicity."

" That is precisely the thought that was in my
own mind," rejoins the clergyman. " It is evidently better that we should find some meeting-
place that shall be neutral ground. One of the

clergymen whom I shall invite is Father Clancy
of St. Patrick's Church; he would hesitate to attend a meeting held in a Protestant church, and
we could ill afford to spare him from our conference.   I am sure that if he is properly approached
he will coöperate with us heartily."

"There is a comfortable little room, large enough
for our purposes, in the rear of my counting-room,"
says Tomlinson.   "I will see that it is put in order
for this meeting, if you desire it.   It is better that
this company should meet privately.   As soon as
our plans are matured the public will be entitled
to know all our purposes, not before."

III

THE company which gathered in Mr. Tomlinson's back office represented very fairly all the
best elements of the population.   Out of a possible fifty-five, thirty-nine were present; the mercan-
tile and professional classes had responded with
some excellent representatives, but Mr. Hathaway
was the only man who brought his full quota of
ten from the ranks of the wage-workers.   There
were, of course, some conspicuous vacancies in
this group.   There was not one saloon-keeper, and
not one ward politician.   Could it be true that
these people expected to govern their city without
any aid from the powers that be?   It must be con-
fessed that to the denizens of the city hall the

aspect of this assembly would have been revolutionary in the extreme.

"If you will come to order, gentlemen," said the clear voice of Mr. Tomlinson, "I will venture, as your host, to make known the purpose of this gathering. Five men who meet from time to time for quite another purpose were forced to confront the fact that this city is sadly misgoverned. In a general way, I suppose, we all believe this, and we make a great many complaints about it; yet as to what the defects of our government are, or how they may be corrected, we may have very confused notions. But it seemed to us five men that we, as citizens, had some duties which we had been neglecting, and we determined to call a few of our neighbors together to consult with us, and to take part with us, if they deem it wise, in a sustained and patient effort to improve the character of our city government. Perhaps I may say that the one man of the five whose ideas on the subject were most clear and mature was Mr. Samuel Hathaway; he represents a class whose interest in good government is as deep as that of any other class, and I am glad to see that it is well represented here to-night. I have the honor to propose that the chair be taken by Mr. Hathaway."

The proposition was greeted with cheers, and Mr. Hathaway blushingly advanced to the post of honor.

"I thank you, gentlemen," he said, in manly fashion, but with a little tremor in his voice, "for

this expression of your kindness. It was some
words of mine upon the value of organization, I
suppose, that Mr. Tomlinson referred to. The
wage-workers of this generation have learned the
power of organization. It is a power that can
be abused, of course. Doubtless it is sometimes
abused; but it is only through the coöperation of
men that rights are secured and justice is estab-
lished. And we are here to-night to try to learn
how to coöperate for the promotion of the best
interests of the community. As capitalists, as
laborers, as professional men, as churchmen, as
Democrats, as Republicans, as Prohibitionists, our
ideas may be unlike, and our interests diverse;
but we are all citizens of this city, and we are all
alike interested in honest, efficient government.
Can we not forget all our other differences and
work together for this end?"

The carpenter's little speech was well received,
and the pride of his fellow-workmen was evidently
touched by the honor accorded to him, and by the
modest and sensible way in which he bore it.

"I will venture," said the chairman, "in the way
of further explaining the project before us, to call
upon Mr. Reginald Payne. Perhaps he may be
able to give us something definite to consider."

"We are here," said Mr. Payne, "for conference
and consultation. Nobody is authorized to present any plans to this meeting. Nobody wishes
to anticipate or define the action to be taken by
this meeting. I have myself no clearly formulated

scheme, but I will simply throw out a few suggestions, with which I hope you will deal frankly. My ideas are briefly these—I have put them down in writing, for clearness and brevity:

"I. There should be an association of citizens for the improvement of municipal government.

"II. It should be a permanent organization, with the expectation of indefinite continuance. We should no more contemplate the termination of its work than that of a church or a college. The time will never come when there will not be need of such an organization, through which municipal patriotism may be fostered and expressed.

"III. The condition of membership should be the signing of a declaration that in municipal affairs party politics should be ignored, and a pledge that the members will, in all these matters, act in independence of the claims of party.

"IV. The work of the association should be: (a) To hold regular meetings for the discussion of topics relating to the welfare of the city, and especially to its government. (b) To collect and publish information upon these topics, including the enforcement or non-enforcement of the laws; the management of the city's finances; the manner in which contracts are made and fulfilled; the conduct of elections; and so forth. (c) To inquire into the methods by which cities are governed, and to see whether it is possible to improve our charter so that our administration shall be more simple and efficient.

"Some such scheme as this has been simmering in my mind. The details may be improved; the whole plan might be improved. I only offer it for consideration."

A brief silence followed Mr. Payne's statement. Judge Hamlin broke it by the question : "Will Mr. Payne stand up again and let us ask him a few questions? Possibly a colloquy of this sort may bring out the points that need to be made clear."

"With pleasure," answered the lawyer; "you can soon find out how little I know."

"Well, then," continued the judge, "tell us whether you would have this association go into politics by nominating candidates for city offices."

"No; my judgment would be against that for the present. I would make it an educational more than a political association. But I would leave it perfectly free to take such action as its members may at any time think wise."

"The party organizations will remain in the field?"

"Undoubtedly."

"And will present candidates for our suffrages at every city election?"

"That may be presumed."

"How much could this association effect, then, in the way of reforming the government? Should we not be obliged to vote for such candidates as the gods of the caucus saw fit to give us?"

"Certainly. I do not expect, as the fruit of our labors, any immediate and radical change in the government of the city. That is the great mistake of the citizens' movements. They go into this business expecting to do it up in six months or so, and make no provision for a long campaign. Their ideas reach no further than the next election. If, in the first contest, they are successful, they imagine that the city is redeemed, and disband their forces; if they are defeated, they assume that the struggle is hopeless, and fling away their weapons. I hope that this enterprise will begin in a different way."

"Precisely what, then, do you expect to accomplish?" persisted the catechist.

"I should hope," replied the lawyer, "that by the constant agitation which we shall keep up, by the facts which we shall bring to light, by the discussion which we shall promote, public opinion would be created and purified, and thus a steady pressure brought to bear upon the managers of both parties, which might induce them to give us better candidates. I have no doubt that we shall be able to present a great many well-attested and undeniable facts which will startle the people of this city, and make them feel that something must be done. I presume that our careful investigation of the methods by which the city's business is managed will show that it is slipshod, wasteful, reckless to the last degree. I believe that we shall be able to suggest important and desirable changes in the form of our municipal organization."

"The enterprise is educational, then, mainly?"

" Yes, mainly. The work of enlightenment and agitation seems to me to be the first and most important work."

Mr. Payne sat down, and there was a moment's silence. It was broken by the voice of one of the clerical contingent, the Reverend Fletcher Frambes, a swarthy man with a bushy brow and a heavy jaw.

"This educational campaign," he said, "may furnish a very interesting amusement to those who take part in it, and it may result in some remote benefits; but I confess that I am somewhat disappointed in the program which has been outlined to us. I was hoping that we should be invited to take hold in a more direct and vigorous way of the existing evils. Everybody knows that our city is terribly misgoverned. The laws for the suppression of vice are practically ignored. In spite of statutes and city ordinances, the saloons are open all night long and all day Sunday; the gamblers do business as openly as the druggists; the houses of infamy hang out their signs. It seems to me that the first thing to do is to enforce the laws against these social abominations. Over in Steelopolis they have a Law and Order League which is making it hot for these lawbreakers. I was in hopes that this conference might be looking toward some such work as this."

"Well, gentlemen," said the lawyer, "this is a fair question which my clerical brother has raised: to what extent is it wise to go into the business of detecting and punishing crime? What Mr. Frambes has said about the disregard of law is quite true; the question is, whether it is wise for us to organize a volunteer association for the enforcement of the laws. That was not my idea; but I should like to hear the opinions of others."

"My opinion," said Judge Hamlin, standing up, and speaking deliberately, "is very clear on this point. Nobody who knows me will doubt that I believe in a strict enforcement of the laws; the classes to which Mr. Frambes refers know where I stand. But I am not in favor of volunteer organizations for the prosecution of lawbreakers. I am aware of what has been done in Steelopolis and in other cities; in some cases, no doubt, temporary gains for morality have been made by such methods; but, as a rule, and in the long run, the effect of such measures will be injurious. We have police authorities, and a police force, whose sworn duty it is to enforce statutes and ordinances. This is their business — their only business. We make a great mistake when we take it out of their hands. The moment we begin to employ detectives, and to engage in the prosecution of any class of offenders, the police will consider themselves discharged of responsibility for this portion of their duty. 'You have undertaken this job,' they will say to us; 'now go ahead with it, and see what you can do.' Of course they will give us no help; most likely they will obstruct our efforts in many secret ways. There is now, in all probability, a pretty good understanding between the police authorities and these classes of lawbreakers. This volunteer detective business is much more likely to strengthen than to weaken this league between the lawbreakers and police. Desultory and spasmodic efforts to prosecute the violators of law will accomplish very little, and when they are abandoned, as they soon will be, we shall be more completely in the hands of the lawless classes than we are to-day. Therefore I put very little trust in these private organizations for the enforcement of law. I know that many excellent people have taken part in them, from the highest of motives; I myself was a member of such an organization in this city several years ago; it was my experience then which convinced me that it is an unwise method. A law-abiding people must intrust the enforcement of its laws to officials chosen and sworn to perform their duty, and must hold them responsible for its performance. It is weak and childish to permit them to neglect their work, and then to take hold and do it for them. If my hostler neglects to keep my stable clean, I am not in the habit of showing my displeasure with him by doing the work myself, and permitting him to sit and smoke on the sidewalk. That method of dealing with employees is just as foolish when they are public officials as when they are private workmen. The only way to get the laws enforced in this city is to compel the men to enforce them whose business it is."

Judge Hamlin's little speech was greeted with applause, in which about half of the company joined. The rest looked doubtful.

"The judge's philosophy is all right," said the minister; "but are we to sit still and see our young men ruined and our homes broken up by these public enemies?"

"No; we are not to sit still," replied the judge; "we are to be up and doing; the only question is, what is the wisest thing to do? We might adopt measures which would yield some temporary gains, as I have said, but which would tend, eventually, to weaken respect for government, and to lower the standards of our public officials. The losses of such a course are greater than the gains. The trouble with most of our attempts at municipal reform has been that we have been content with making a raid, now and then, into the territory of the lawbreakers and the corruptionists; and when we have cast out one devil, we have gone our ways to our stores and our offices, and seven others worse than the first have returned and entered in. We have got to think and plan for radical and permanent reform. We must have a government worthy of respect, and we must respect it. We must have an efficient government, and require it to prove its efficiency. We must have a responsible government, and hold it to its strict responsibility. It is our business, as citizens, to select capable employees, and to see that they do their duty. It is not our business to do their duty for them. The people are the sovereigns, and they must behave themselves sovereignly. They lower their dignity, and cripple their authority, when they palter, after this manner, with perfidious and insubordinate servants."

The judge spoke with warmth, and the applause was prompt and pretty nearly unanimous.

" Well," answered Mr. Frambes, " I wish to do nothing unwise, and Judge Hamlin's words seem to me reasonable, in the main. I am ready to cooperate with any movement that promises to give us better government."

" But how are we to enlist the people in this enterprise?" inquired one of the newcomers. "The reform of this municipality can be wrought only by the coöperation of the majority of its citizens. Here are thirty or forty of us. By what multiplier can we increase our number to ten thousand?"

"I do not think," answered Principal Harper, " that we shall do well to be in haste about increasing our numbers. The time may come when we shall wish to recruit our ranks, but that is not the first concern. I happen to have in my pocket a pamphlet treating, in a very judicious manner, this whole problem, from which I beg leave to read a paragraph :

" 'The formation of large citizen reform associations, certainly, as an opening wedge to reform, is of questionable value. In such energy is apt to be dissipated, and a sense of individual responsibility lost. Moreover, the way is then opened for

3

the very politicians whom it is designed to dis-
courage to capture the organization and use its
prestige to shield themselves. The best beginning
is made by a few enthusiasts, enrolling as much
influence as possible, devoting themselves to the
study of evils, and the theories and practice elsewhere of purifying local politics and regenerating
municipalities. This little company should be
thoroughly non-partizan, though much of the
best work must be done by working through
party primaries. When the organization has ac-
quired a local standing it may enlarge its membership, and declare its indorsement or disapproval
of individual candidates for local office. But by
agitation, and by education of citizens in the principles on which local government rests, is the best
work done. Needed radical changes in the local
constitution may be thus accomplished, and the
municipality started afresh on approved lines.
This has already been done in a number of cities.'

" I am not quite sure," Mr. Harper continued,
"about all these suggestions; but the principal
contention — that better work can be done in the
educational way by a small association than by a
large one — appears to be reasonable. When I
look round upon this picked company, it seems to
me that we have a force fairly adequate to the
work in hand. I would urge the attendance of
those already invited who are not present; I
would not exclude other desirable persons who
may wish to join our league; but I would invite

no more just now. Most of us have a great deal
to learn. If we desire to fit ourselves for wise
leadership of this movement, we must know far
more than we now do of existing conditions, and
of the best methods of improving them; and this
study of the problem will be best prosecuted, not
in mass meetings, but in small, select, and man-
ageable companies."

"But how," pursued this interlocutor, "would
you get the results of your study into the public
mind?"

"That," answered the schoolmaster, "is a very
important matter, and one to which we may well
give immediate attention. In the first place, I
would have all the meetings of the league public
meetings. The reporters should be notified and
welcomed. The results of our study should be
embodied, so far as possible, not in offhand
speeches, but in crisp, condensed, keenly written
papers, which the newspapers will be glad to print
in full. The discussions following these papers
are likely to be fully reported. I think that this
company embodies intelligence and wit enough to
furnish this community some mighty interesting
reading, and character enough to make its published statements very influential. It will be seen
at once that we are not seeking any partizan advantage; that we are students investigating in a
scientific spirit the conditions of our municipal
life; that we are public-spirited citizens seeking
the welfare of the city, and not looking for office.

I believe that we can do a great deal in a short time toward correcting and reforming and vitalizing public opinion."

"What the principal has said about the scientific spirit," interposed Mr. Morison, "has put an idea into my mind. Would it not be well to organize our league in sections, as the scientific associations are organized, assigning to each section some specific branch of inquiry and investigation ?"

"That was exactly my thought," answered Mr. Payne. "I had put down here on a piece of paper a sketch of such a subdivision. To one section I would assign for study the Police and the Fire Department; to another, Streets and Sewers; to another, the Schools; to another, Poor Relief and Sanitation; to another, Light and Water; to another, Transportation; and to another, all questions relating to Charter Reform. Let there be a committee of three in charge of each of these sections; let every member of the league join himself to the section in which he can be most useful; and let the chairmen of these seven committees be the executive committee of the league."

"Excellent," responded the rector. "This looks like business. And now, Mr. Chairman, let me propose a committee, consisting of Mr. Payne, Mr. Harper, and yourself, to put this organization into form, nominate officers, and report at a subsequent meeting."

The motion was unanimously agreed to, and underscored with applause.

"There is one more question," said the lawyer, "on which your committee may need instruction. It is assumed that we shall have regular meetings. How often shall we meet?"

"Once a month is often enough for a public meeting," answered Mr. Morison. "The sections will wish to meet more frequently. Let them arrange that for themselves."

"I doubt," said Mr. Tomlinson, "whether once a month will do the work. I understand why the parson, whose evenings are nearly all occupied, should prefer monthly meetings; but it seems to me that if we wish to make upon this community the impression that we ought to make, we must meet every week. The parson knows—at any rate, some of his professional brethren know — the value of continuous impression. If you want to heat the iron by hammering, you must not only strike hard, you must strike often. The same thing is true of all efforts to arouse popular interest. The attention of the people must be held to the subject; you must keep the matter hot in their minds. It seems to me that it would be well to have only one of these sections report at each meeting. That gives each committee seven weeks to prepare its report; it can be fully digested, and sharply presented, and the people will have one subject to think about for that week."

"I quite agree with my neighbor," answered Judge Hamlin. "This is no holiday business which we have undertaken. It means hard work, persistent work, self-denying work. It will involve sacrifice of leisure, loss of sleep, and the postponement or neglect of other interests that are by no means unimportant. Our friends, the clergymen, have many weekly engagements which they consider sacred and binding; I do not disparage their work when I say that they can find no better use for one evening in the week than to devote it to this cause."

"My friend the manufacturer, and my neighbor the judge," said Mr. Morison, "do me a little less than justice if they intimate that I do not apprehend the relative importance of the work in which we have enlisted. My parishioners are not likely to make any such mistake. I have harped upon this string until they are weary. Very well do I understand that the one influence which stands in most deadly opposition to all that the church of God is trying to do in the community is that of our city government. By its notorious complicity with vice; by the official indorsement and continuance that it gives to the worst forms of evil; by the shameless dishonesties which are charged against its administration, and of which in the popular judgment it stands convicted; by the cynical contempt for their oaths of office which many of its officials manifest; by what it does, and by what it fails to do, this municipal government of ours is a great foe of morality in this community. It is a hard thing to say, but it is not recklessly said; after much careful thought I am forced to say it. Our studies and investigations will, I trust, bring home to the people of this city some of the facts on which this judgment is based. No one present is likely to estimate more highly than I do the gravity of the interests with which we are dealing. I was thinking of others rather than of myself when I proposed a monthly meeting, and I am more than willing to give one evening in a week to this work."

"There is one other question," said one of the working-men, "which I will make bold to raise. Some of these municipal clubs, as I happen to know, are rather expensive affairs. We working-men would be glad to bear our part in this one; but if we are members, we wish to be on an equality with the rest, and we can't stand the fees and dues which are often charged."

"That is an important suggestion," answered Mr. Tomlinson; "I hope that the committee will consider it well. Some expense will necessarily be incurred, but I trust that it will be made as light as possible, so that men with small incomes may, without burdening themselves, be able to meet the obligations of membership."

"The principal expense," answered Mr. Payne, "will be the rent of a room for our meetings. The committee will endeavor to find a suitable room at the lowest possible rent."

"If this room will serve your purpose," Mr. Tomlinson ventured, "you are welcome to it."

The manufacturer's generous offer was greeted
with applause, and the meeting adjourned, to as-
semble in the same place on the next Saturday
evening.

IV

IT could hardly be supposed that such a meeting
as has now been reported could be kept an entire
secret in a city like Cosmopolis. The reporters
soon got wind of it, and several of the gentlemen
who were present were subjected to interviews,
through which the people of the city were pretty
well informed of all that had taken place. The
composite character of the assembly, representing
as it did both parties and all sorts and conditions
of citizens, excited much comment; no similar
combination had ever before been effected; people wondered by what charm such a group had
been collected. The denizens of the city hall jeered
at it as "Bill Tomlinson's happy family"; but,
though they made light of it, they were evidently
rather solemnized by the apparition. It was likely
that these people would soon be asking disagreeable questions and publishing annoying statements, and they were inclined to resent such interference. This was a method of attack to which
they were not accustomed, and they were at a loss
to know how it could best be met. They had been

disturbed now and then by impulsive attempts on the part of reputable people to get possession of the primaries and to control the nominations for city officers, and by occasional attempts to run a citizens' ticket; and they knew perfectly well how to neutralize or defeat all such political assaults. But these people, who seemed to be bent on getting possession of the facts respecting their administration of the city government, and on keeping these facts before the people, were fighting with a weapon which they did not know how to parry. Herr Schwab, the minister of finance at the city hall, was highly indignant when he heard what was on foot. "Dose infernal sbies!" he vociferated, "let dem come a-sdickin' dere noses into my pizness, off dey tare. I 'll gick de first man of dem de sdairs down!"

"Betther think twice about that, me hearty," said O'Halloran, blandly. "That w'u'd make a foine thriple-header for our young friend the reporter. Ye 'd be playin' into their hands quite too cleverly. Betther howld yer temper, and circumvent them by sthrategy."

Precisely what manner of strategy Mr. O'Halloran proposed was not at once divulged; but it was evident that the club would not be furthered in its investigations by the authorities at the city hall.

The adjourned meeting of the club, on the next Saturday evening, showed an increased attendance. The form of organization, substantially as agreed upon, was reported and adopted; Judge Hamlin was made the president of the club, Sam Hathaway its vice-president, and Mr. Tomlinson its treasurer; the seven committees were constituted, and the machinery was declared to be in running order. The president, whose provisional acceptance of the office had evidently been secured beforehand, was ready with a well-prepared inaugural address, which was intended, no doubt, to strike the key-note of this campaign of education. Some of the points of his speech are worth transferring to this report. It is better to extract them than to condense them:

"The business before us," said Judge Hamlin, "is perhaps the most serious business which Americans now have upon their hands. The population of our cities is rapidly increasing, and the government of our cities is, as a general rule, inefficient and corrupt — in the words of Mr. James Bryce, 'the one conspicuous failure of the United States.' Ex-President White is not speaking too strongly when he asserts that 'the city governments of the United States are the worst in Christendom — the most expensive, the most inefficient, and the most corrupt.' Reasons for this failure may easily be found. We shall find them in the course of these studies. I will only refer to a few of the more important.

"The rapid growth of our cities has thrown upon us great problems of engineering and physical construction for which we were wholly unprepared. Corruption and jobbery have flourished upon our inexperience.

"The problems of social construction have been complicated in the same way. A form of government which answered fairly well in a large village, or a city of ten or twenty thousand, becomes utterly inadequate when the population rises to scores or hundreds of thousands. You might as well undertake to manage the street traffic of New York with the ancient omnibus as to govern some of our cities under their present charters.

"The municipal problem has been muddled by legislative interference. The municipal corporation has been defined by the United States Courts as a 'subordinate branch of the governmental power of the State'; it is regarded as a creature of the legislature; and what the legislature has made, it may at any time reconstruct or destroy. In many of our States the legislatures have constantly interfered with the administration of municipalities, sometimes with benevolent intention, often with sinister purpose, almost always with mischievous result. The members of the legislature do not understand the problems of municipal organization; a majority of them have no interests involved, and can be held in no way responsible for their action. It would be putting it too strongly to say that the legislature should have no power to interfere with the government of cities, but it is becoming evident that this power should be sharply restricted by constitutional provisions.

" The foreign population is often charged with
the miscarriages of municipal government. No
doubt this cause must be well studied. The social
habits of large classes reared in other lands make
the enforcement of liquor laws and Sunday laws
difficult ; and the disregard of these laws weakens
in these people, and in natives as well, the whole-
some sentiment of respect for law in general. My
own opinion is that the people of the United States,
native-born and foreign-born, have received an
education in lawlessness through the feeble and
futile handling of the liquor laws which it will
take them a great many years to unlearn. I do not
hesitate to say that it would have been infinitely
better for this country if there had been, during the
last fifty years, no legal restriction at all upon the
manufacture and sale of intoxicating liquors. I do
not believe that there would have been any more
intemperance than there has been, and I am quite
sure that we should see far less of that wide-spread
contempt for law which is one of the alarming
symptoms of our municipal disorder. This state
of things is due, to a considerable extent, to the
presence of the foreign elements in our population.
It goes without saying, also, that the attempts of
these people, who have had very little education
under free institutions, to take part in the government of our cities must often have resulted
disastrously ; while the demagogue finds his oppor-
tunity among such ignorant voters. Still, I am not
disposed to put quite so much emphasis upon this

cause as some critics do. The great mass of the foreigners are industrious, thrifty, law-abiding people; they might be trained to good citizenship if we would give our minds to the business. They need a great deal of political education, and we have left that task mainly to the ward heelers and the spoilsmen. I do not think that American citizens are entitled to say very much about the failure of the foreigners to bear their part wisely in our public affairs. We might have withheld the suffrage from them; but when we gave it, we ought to have known that we took upon ourselves the responsibility of training them to use it. This involves a vast deal of hard work, and we have shirked the work. Why should we blame them for failing in a function for which they have had no preparation? If you should turn a force of raw hands into a shoe-factory, to run the machinery and to carry on the manufacture with little or no instruction, you would not be greatly surprised if the output were meager and poor and if the machinery were wrecked and ruined. Something like this is what we have done with our foreign voters, and it strikes me that we are rather unjust when we throw upon them, so largely as we are inclined to do, the fault of the failure of our municipal government.

"The last reason of this failure which I shall mention is the neglect of their duty by those citizens who are the natural leaders of society. The educated men, the professional men, the active business men of our cities, are the men to whom the political leadership of the community belongs; we shall never have good government until these men come to the front and take hold of it. You might just as well expect the human body to be an efficient servant of the mind with its eyes put out and its hands cut off, as to expect the body politic to perform its functions properly when these classes practically exclude themselves from all part in the government. That these classes have neglected their duty as citizens is too palpable to need proof. 'The great mass of so-called "best citizens,"' says a moderate writer, 'have no sympathy with local affairs; they want no office; they refuse to take it when offered. They wash their hands of responsibility. There were, it is estimated, 100,000 citizens of New York city who in 1890 failed to register, and of those registered about 43,000 failed to vote. Of the 266,000 voters in New York city in 1885 but 201,000 voted, and of these but from 20,000 to 25,000, it is estimated, went to the primaries. The alarming part of it is that these heedless ones are in great measure the citizens of intelligence and character, whose votes are needed to nullify the votes of the ignorant and irresponsible, whom political workers never fail to muster at the polls.'

"How true, also, are these words of Mr. Bryce: 'In America, as everywhere else in the world, the commonwealth suffers more from apathy and short-sightedness in the upper classes, who ought to lead, than from ignorance or recklessness in the humbler classes, who are generally ready to follow when they are wisely and patriotically led.' And the excuses made for their neglect only aggravate the guilt of it. It is the offense which these delicate and fastidious gentlemen fear to suffer in their feelings, so they say, which leads them to keep out of the political arena. They do not enjoy contact with rough, uncultivated, not always savory crowds. They have been jostled in the caucuses; they have been jeered at by persons who do not use good grammar; they feel that their superior intelligence is not properly recognized by the political bosses. Sometimes they have attempted, singly, or in squads of two or three, to take part in the primaries; naturally they have accomplished very little, and they have abandoned politics as a hopeless field of effort. I must say that I regard this excuse as very largely false and hypocritical. I do not believe that these persons have suffered half so much as they pretend to have suffered from the disagreeable incidents of political campaigning. All this unpleasantness is greatly exaggerated. The real reason why these gentlemen neglect their political duties is, in nine cases out of ten, because they are too selfish, too sordid to give attention to them; because they are unwilling to sacrifice their financial and professional interests to the extent which is required in a thorough and faithful performance of the duties of citizenship. The blight upon our municipal patriotism is what President White calls 'mercantilism.' It is a hard thing to say, but I believe that it is true. It matters not, however, which is the real cause of this neglect. Either explanation is sufficiently shameful. It is a despicable soul which can take refuge in either of them. Not for such dainty fingers or such itching palms are the great privileges of American citizenship.

"I trust, gentlemen, that this club may do something to awaken in the minds of our citizens the sentiment of municipal patriotism. These local interests with which we are to deal are not less important, not less vital, than those interests of which the National Government is the custodian. Indeed, the very foundation of national welfare is laid in the right ordering of the life of our towns and cities. The nation can no more prosper while its local communities are badly governed than a tree can prosper while its several branches are covered with nests of worms and blight. Our first political duty is to give this city a good system of government. We must not look to the legislature; we must give the legislature very distinctly to understand that we insist on governing ourselves; that it will be dangerous business to impose upon this city a form of government which is not acceptable to its citizens. There is intelligence enough in this city to govern the city, and it must be summoned to the task. The men whose business it is to govern it, and who have neglected their business, must be made ashamed of their neglect, and must bring forth fruits meet for repentance.

"One more remark will, I trust, be pardoned. We are to study the municipal problem in all its bearings. We shall be compelled to investigate the current administration. We are going to find out all the facts, and to publish them. Let this investigation be conducted in a perfectly judicial temper. Let us be careful to make no statements for which we have not abundant proof. Let us content ourselves, for the most part, with pointing out the facts, and avoiding objurgatory comments. The confidence of this community in our conclusions will be secured by cautious, moderate, colorless statements. We shall be brought into constant contact with the city officials. They must be made to understand that our object is to co-operate with them in the discharge of their duty; to raise no unjust prejudice against them ; to put no hindrances in their way so long as they are engaged in the administration of their offices. We shall be glad to find, in any case, that these affairs are honestly and efficiently administered. We shall be ready to give the full meed of approval to any official who shows himself mindful of his oath and his honor. We do not propose to meddle with any man who is doing his duty. But we are entitled, as citizens, as the responsible rulers of this community, to know whether our employees are doing their duty or not; and we are determined to find out. If they are not doing their duty, we mean to know why. It may be that they are crippled or embarrassed by bad forms of organization. It may be that their failure is largely due to the poor tools which we have furnished them. If so, we must

4

give them better tools. But whatever the reason may be, we are going to bring it to the light of day. In this effort all right-minded officials will coöperate with us. From the sort that is otherwise minded, and from all their political associates, we may expect unstinted abuse and unscrupulous misrepresentation. I trust that we are not so thin-skinned as to flinch from our duty on this account. We have a great work to do, the difficulty and disagreeableness of which are largely the fruit of our own neglect. Let us try to make amends for past remissness by the courage, fidelity, and persistence with which we prosecute the task which we have all too tardily undertaken."

The inaugural address of Judge Hamlin was frequently punctuated with cheers, and its vigorous conclusion was greeted with prolonged applause.

After an announcement by the executive committee that the next meeting would be devoted to perfecting the organization, that the committees in charge of the several sections would be expected to report in the order of their appointment, and that the first report would be called for in two weeks from the committee on the Police and the Fire Department, the club adjourned.

CHAPTER II

THE CLUB GETS TO WORK

V

THE first business meeting of the Cosmopolis City Club was well advertised. The newspapers had published in full the inaugural address of Judge Hamlin, and had discussed it thoroughly; several citizens had joined in the newspaper debate in letters addressed to the editors, and the program of the club had been the subject of general conversation. The newspapers of the party then in possession of the city offices were, of course, skeptical and querulous; evidently they meant to make the path of the club as thorny as possible; but inasmuch as Judge Hamlin belonged to their party, and was a man of great influence in its councils, they were constrained to veil their hostility. The opposition journals were, of course, equally ready to make capital for their party out of the investigation; and they gleefully pointed out to the club directions in which its studies could be pushed with profit.

Meanwhile the committee in charge of the first section had been diligently at work getting at the

facts respecting the administration of the Police
and the Fire Departments, and the officials of these
departments had been considerably stirred up by
the knowledge that their affairs were to have an
airing. A number of them were present to hear
the report of the committee. The room of the club
was densely packed with interested auditors, and
the reporters' tables were surrounded by a strong
force of recording angels with sharpened pencils
and expectant countenances.

The chairman of the first section was our old
friend Harper, principal of the Central High
School. His report was written with clearness and
pith, and was read with the utmost deliberation
and calmness of tone; but the suppressed inten-
sity of some passages was extremely telling. There
was an occasional symptom of applause, but the
president promptly checked it, the unrestrained
laughter of the audience at some of the keen statements being the only audible demonstration.

According to their report the committee had
found that the Fire Department was in good condition, well manned, well officered, well administered; the discipline was excellent, the service effective. The chief had made them welcome, and
had given them every facility for the prosecution
of their inquiries. As a working force the department was unexcelled, and the men were evidently
proud of the record which they had made for
themselves. Certain transactions in the purchase
of engines, and in the erection of new engine-

houses, awaited further investigation; for these, however, the chief and his subordinates were in no way responsible. The committee had only praise for the administration of this important branch of the municipal service.

With respect to the Police Department, it could be truthfully said that certain classes of crimes— all crimes against property, and the graver offenses against the rights of the person — were eagerly detected and sharply prosecuted. Pickpockets, sneak thieves, and burglars were summarily dealt with, and actual or intending murderers were made to feel the force of the law.

But certain classes of offenses against the law seemed to be wholly ignored by the officers of the law. There was a city ordinance, which the committee recited, by which all the drinking-places of the city were required to close at midnight. This was not a musty ordinance; it was enacted only two years before, but no attempt was made to enforce it. The committee had spent the best part of several nights in personally investigating the manner of its non-enforcement; they had themselves heard liquor called for, and had seen it sold, after midnight, in ninety-five places, of which they had a list that would be published in the newspapers. The relations of the police to these violators of law appeared to be intimate and cordial. The committee had frequently seen policemen standing at the doors of these open saloons, and talking with persons passing in and out: in four cases they had seen policemen standing at the bar with glasses in their hands; they had the numbers of these policemen, and would publish them also.

There was also a city ordinance forbidding the sale of liquors on Sundays. This ordinance was of the same date as the midnight-closing ordinance. Behind it was a statute, first enacted by the legislature more than forty years ago, but re-enacted, in one form or another, twice or thrice within the last ten years, by which the selling of intoxicating liquors on the first day of the week, commonly called Sunday, was made a misdemeanor, and all police officers were required to arrest and prosecute such offenders. To this law and this ordinance no respect was paid. All the drinking-places in the city were wide open on Sunday, with no effort at concealment; the relation of the police to this form of lawlessness was precisely the same as to the other.

Houses of prostitution and assignation were numerous; they had adopted various devices for advertising themselves; some portions of the city had been rendered uninhabitable by their presence, and respectable families had been compelled to sacrifice their homes because of the encroachments of these evil habitations. Now and then one of these places was raided, but it was uniformly the least popular and successful among them which suffered; many of the best known and most frequented of these resorts of vice had enjoyed com-

plete immunity for a long period. It was, of
course, absurd to say that the policemen did not
know of these places; and the committee had seen
many indications that they were regarded by the
police as under their protection. One or two patrolmen who had manifested an unfriendly disposition
toward them had been transferred to other beats.
The committee had evidence on these points, which
would be furnished if their statement was questioned.

The State laws forbidding gambling were ex-
plicit and stringent. The committee made several
quotations from these statutes. One section expressly commanded the superintendent of police
in every city, on reasonable suspicion that any
place was used for gambling purposes, to raid the
premises, to arrest all persons found in them, and
to confiscate and destroy all gambling apparatus.
In the face of these laws, gambling was carried on
with small pretense of concealment. The committee had ascertained the location of eighteen public
gambling-rooms; various members of the committee had visited all these rooms, and had found
no difficulty in gaining admittance; they had seen
gambling games in progress in every one of them.
The position of the police authorities with respect
to criminals of this class might be inferred from an
interview, published in one of the city newspapers,
with one of the recently chosen police commissioners. Being asked what policy he should advocate
with respect to gambling, this commissioner was

reported as saying that he should be in favor of
"a conservative policy." His further remarks indicated that he was in favor of "conserving" the
gambling-places, or at any rate the most popular and successful among them. He said that he
doubted whether gambling could be entirely extirpated, and thought it better to have a few respectable and well-known places, which could be watched
by the police, than to have the business driven
into holes and corners. A suit, which had been
brought in one of the courts since the committee was appointed, had shown that another of the
police commissioners was part owner of a saloon,
which was also a notorious gambling-place. Another incident, fully reported in the newspapers,
threw further light upon the relation of the police
to the gamblers. One of the most disreputable of
the Sunday newspapers undertook to blackmail the
proprietor of a gambling-place. The gambler bit
at the bait, agreed to submit to the extortion, appointed a meeting in his own room with the editor,
and paid over the hush-money demanded. Immediately on the editor's receipt of the money, several
policemen came forth from their concealment in
the gambler's rooms, arrested the editor, and threw
him into prison, where he still was languishing.
The gambler, of course, had his money restored
to him, and his business did not suffer interruption
for a single night. These facts, which were beyond
questioning, seemed to make it unnecessary for
the committee to make any inquiry of the police

commissioners, or of the chief of police, respecting their purposes or their policy. It seemed to
the committee, however, that it might be well for
them to ascertain, so far as they could, to what
extent public opinion sanctioned these methods
of dealing with offenses against the law. They
took considerable pains to arrive at safe conclusions upon this matter, and then requested an
interview with the police authorities. In order
that no injustice might be done in the report of
this interview, one of their number, who was an
expert stenographer, took notes of the conversation, and the committee offered his affidavit that
the report submitted was accurate and complete. As showing the state of mind of these custodians of the public peace, portions of this conversation were recited. Our narrative would not
be complete without them.

There were present Messrs. Harper, Paterson,
and Hastings of the committee; Commissioners Dugan, Murphy, Benson, and Schneider, and
Superintendent O'Kane.

Dugan.— Well, gentlemen, what can we do for
you?

Harper.— My friends and I are here to ask a
few questions, for our own information, with respect to the administration of the Police Department.

Dugan.— What business have you with the
Police Department, and what right have you to be
prying into our affairs?

Harper.—We are citizens of Cosmopolis, and taxpayers; we are interested in the efficiency of the Police Department, because our lives and property are insecure if the police are incapable and untrustworthy. We have heard many complaints against this branch of our municipal government, and we have determined to find out for ourselves whether they are true. We suppose that we have a right to know, and that it is our business to know, whether the men to whom we have intrusted this important service are faithfully performing it.

Dugan.—You 've heard a lot of lies, of course; you 'd better not believe all you hear.

Harper.—We intend to believe nothing for which we have not good evidence. We have taken nothing upon hearsay; it is only that which we have seen with our own eyes which we wish to have you explain to us.

Dugan.—What 's that?

Harper.—You are aware, doubtless, of the existence of ordinances and laws requiring the closing of liquor-shops after midnight and on Sunday.

Dugan.—Well?

Harper.—You are also aware that these places are open all night and all day Sunday.

Dugan.—Don't admit nothing of the sort. Orders was issued two years ago to have 'em shut up, and they have n't been countermanded.

Harper.—Do you not know, gentlemen, that these orders are disregarded continually by hundreds of liquor-sellers?

Murphy.— No; we don't know any such thing.

Harper.— Possibly Superintendent O'Kane can enlighten you?

O'Kane.— Well, I suppose that there are a few restaurants that keep open nights and Sundays, but I don't think that there is much violation.

Harper.— The superintendent is, I suppose, a man of steady habits, and always goes to bed at an early hour. Let me give him a little information. I have here a list of ninety-five places which we, who are before you, have found open after midnight and on Sunday, and in which we have heard intoxicating liquors called for, and have seen them sold at unlawful hours.

Benson.— Well, gentlemen, what of it? It is no use beating about the bush; you know perfectly well that these laws have n't been enforced for many a day, and that they are not going to be. Nobody wants them to be enforced but a small handful of Prohibition cranks.

Hastings.— Are you quite sure of that?

Benson.— Of course I am; every man of common sense knows it.

Hastings.— I am not a Prohibitionist, nor a total abstainer; I believe that liquor ought to be sold under proper regulations; but I do not think that the saloons should be open nights and Sundays.

Benson.— I don't care what you think. I know that the people of the city, with a very few exceptions, are in favor of a liberal policy in dealing with this business.

Harper.— How do you know ?

Benson.—Just as any man knows anything —
by the use of my common sense.

Harper.— I must doubt whether any man can
be absolutely sure, by the use of his own common
sense, of what his neighbor's opinions would be
on a subject of this nature.   At any rate, we have
not thought it safe to trust our own impressions
without putting some foundations of fact under
them.   Accordingly, we selected two long streets
in this city,— Poplar street and South street,—
the one mainly occupied with the residences of
the wealthier class, the other with the homes of
working-men.   We sent circulars to all the residents upon these two streets, asking them these
three questions: 1. "Are you in favor of closing
the saloons at midnight?"   2. "Are you in favor of closing the saloons on Sunday?"   3. "Are
you in favor of the suppression of the gambling-
places?"   Of the 204 residents of Poplar street
176 responded, and of these 158 answered our first
question in the affirmative.   Of the 316 residents
of South street 243 responded, and 209 of these
answered the same question in the same way.   We
believe that these are representative localities;
and an overwhelming majority of the residents of
these localities have expressed themselves as in
favor of the enforcement of these laws.   Our opinion is, that the whole city, if polled, would give
substantially the same answer to this question.
We can think of no reason why the people of

these two streets should differ essentially from
the people of other portions of the city. Can you?
[No answer.]

Harper.— We may also claim to know, not by
"common sense," but by some careful observa-
tion, that the class of people who frequent the all-
night saloon is a very small class, when compared
with the population of this city. It is not the
business men whom we find there; it is not the
clerks and employees of our business houses, except an occasional black sheep among them; it is
not, to any great extent, the working-men: it is a
small class of idle, dissolute, disorderly persons,
who are close upon the borders of crime and pau-
perism. These are the principal patrons of the
all-night saloon. Do the police commissioners
think it worth while to keep these places open for
the benefit of this class?
[No answer.]

Harper.— Have the commissioners undertaken
to discover what the saloon-keepers themselves
have to say about it?

Murphy.— I know that a few of them would be
willing to close, if the rest would do so.

Harper.— We have addressed inquiries to all
whose names are found in the city directory; and
of these one third — including nearly all of those
which may be considered "respectable"— reply
that they would be glad to have the law enforced.

Dugan.— Well, gentlemen, we are much obliged
to you for taking so much pains to enlighten us;

we 'll think the matter over, and see what can be done.

Harper.—Thank you. And I wish that the commissioners, if they are not satisfied, would take pains to inform themselves as to the facts in the case. Permit me also, before we go, to give you the result of our inquiry upon the other questions. With respect to Sunday closing, the majorities are not so large. Of the 419 replies received 250 were in favor of closing, and 169 were opposed to it. With respect to the enforcement of the gambling laws, there was practical unanimity. Of the 419 answers 407 were affirmative. We are sure that there can be no doubt about the wishes of the great mass of the people respecting this class of offenses against the laws.

Benson.—Well, then, why don't you make complaints yourselves? You say that you have got the names of eighteen men who keep gambling-places. Why don't you go before a justice, and swear out a warrant, and have them arrested?

Harper.— Because, gentlemen, that is not our business. It is your business. The law expressly commands you to do it. We should be interfering in your business in a very improper manner if we did any such thing. It is perfectly proper for us to bring you information; it is neither good law nor good business policy for us to take your work out of your hands.

Murphy.—Before you go, gentlemen, let me say that I 'm a good deal astonished at what you 've been telling us. I may as well own up that I did not think things were in just such shape. I 'm a pretty busy man, and I don't know so much as I ought to know about what is going on in the city. Brother Dugan here was a little sarcastic when he said that he was obliged to you ; but I *am* obliged to you; that 's honest; and I 'll do what I can to bring about a better state of things.

Schneider.—Well, I 'll say the same. I don't know just what to believe. Folks are always saying that these laws is just dead letters, and that we 've no call to enforce 'em; but if it is not so, then, I suppose — well, I don't know — I 'll think about it.

So ended the interview of the committee with the commissioners. The closing words of Mr. Harper's report may as well be reproduced:

"The mind of the average police commissioner is not easily explored. Doubtless several causes contribute to produce that state of moral inertia in the presence of crime in which we frequently find him. He is not apt to be a person of much intellectual breadth; he is generally subject to the influences that are nearest; and in his immediate surroundings there is not much to quicken his sense of obligation to the community at large. The sentiment of this circle in which he moves is, of course, strongly adverse to restraints of any sort upon vice or disorder. He easily comes to regard this as the sentiment of the whole community; he is unable to keep himself in touch with the

sober and industrious classes. Sometimes, when
there is no intention of malfeasance, he is the
victim of his own near-sightedness.

"Sometimes, beyond question, his inaction is
determined by more sinister influences. The lawless and disorderly classes have votes, and they
are not apt to cast them without a definite consideration. The men whom they elect — and they
generally hold the balance of power — are pledged
to grant them immunity. The shrewdest of these
men, however, are likely to levy tribute upon
them. The committee has no proof to offer and
no charges to make; the committee believe that
many of the officers and men of our police force
are unbribable; but the language of a careful in-
vestigator in another city is probably applicable
here: 'There is, and has long been, a suspicion,
amounting almost to moral certainty, in the minds
of some at least of the citizens engaged in efforts
to enforce law by suppressing vice, that one or
more police captains, and a considerable number
of patrolmen, derive a revenue from shutting their
eyes to what it is not to their interest to see.'

"Another phenomenon to which we are compelled to call attention is the singular insensibility,
on the part of officers of this class, to the ordinary
sentiments of honor, in connection with the taking
of an oath. These men swear that they will respect
and enforce the laws of the city and of the State.
That is the particular business for which they are
employed, and for which they are paid. They are

not understood to be legislators, with the power
to make or repeal law, or judges with the power
of determining its constitutionality; they are simply executive officers, whose duty it is to take the
laws as they are, and to enforce them without fear
or favor. Instead of this we find them, very generally, in this and in other cities, selecting the
laws which they will enforce, and exercising a
discretion as to how much of their duty they will
do, this being a matter with which they are not
intrusted, and which their oath of office expressly
denies to them. Men who solemnly swear that
they will enforce the laws, often turn about, with
the words upon their lips, and denounce their
neighbors for demanding that the laws be enforced. A man may refuse to accept an office of
this kind; but when he accepts it, and receives its
emoluments, and swears to perform its duties, it is
strange that he can so lightly regard his oath of
office. A military officer regards himself as in
honor bound to obey the rules of the service, and
to execute the orders with which he is charged; a
police officer, in the large majority of cases, con-
sults his own convenience and his own interest in
determining whether or not he will do the things
that he has solemnly sworn to do. These remarks
do not apply so much to patrolmen as to commissioners and superintendents. By what means the
moral standards of these men have become so de-
graded. it is not needful to consider; but it is well
to call the attention of the community to the fact

5

that at the very point in our system of laws where
honor is most needed honor is most wanting. This
is a radical defect which must, at whatever cost, be
remedied."

The reading of this report was followed by a
silence which was much more impressive than any
comment could have been. Such an unveiling of
the methods and sentiments of the custodians of
the peace of the city could not fail to awaken reflection. Mr. Tomlinson was first to speak:

"It strikes me," he said, "that the situation
would be ludicrous if it were not intolerable. An
insignificant minority of our population seems to
own and control our police authorities, and the
rest of us sit and grin. The standards of urban
morality are set by the keepers of low dives and
gambling-dens. Even the better class of saloon-
keepers are not 'in it,' as it would seem. What
are we going to do about it?"

"We are going," said Mr. Harper, "to submit
our case to the people. We are going to ask the
newspapers to print our report, and we trust that
the people will read it. If any man thinks that we
have misreported or misrepresented the facts we
hope that he will say so, and we shall be more than
willing to go over the case with him more fully.
If what we have said is true, the people should
know how to apply the remedy. We leave it to
them."

The report of this meeting in the newspapers
the next day was the talk of the town. There

were some querulous and spiteful comments in the
newspapers of the party in power, but they made
little impression; against such clean, scientific
work as that of the committee their diatribes were
ridiculously ineffective. The police authorities
appeared to be divided; Dugan and Benson were
non-committal, Murphy was inclined to favor a
more active policy, and Schneider was in an un-
comfortable state of mind. His honor the mayor,
who was a member of the police commission, but
was absent at the hearing, declined to express any
opinion. Rumors of disputes in the board reached
the public; but days and weeks passed by, and
nothing was done.

VI

MEANTIME the work of the club went steadily
forward. The committee on Streets and Sewers
made its report at the second regular meeting, and
it was full of startling revelations. The paving
contracts for the last three years had been carefully looked into, and the facts and figures presented were clear proof of corruption. It was
shown, beyond question, that certain favored contractors secured all the work, and that other responsible firms had found it useless to compete.
Expert testimony proved that the profit on most
of these contracts amounted to fully forty per
cent. It was shown that in a neighboring city a
far better pavement of the same sort had been laid

at two thirds of the cost of the Cosmopolis pavement. A break in one of the sewers had been repaired during the year, and the committee furnished an itemized statement of the cost of the job. As a sample of the neat manner in which this report was written, a few extracts are subjoined:

" Mr. B. R. Allen was first put in charge, and superintended the excavation, shoring up, and preparation of the bed for the bricklayers. For some unexplained reason Mr. Allen was relieved on September 14, after completing the preliminary work at a cost of $2444.68. The job was then put into the hands of Mr. P. A. Charles. In his payroll, an item of $19,690.62, we find Mr. Charles personally entered for 100 days, Sundays included, as superintendent at $10.00 per day. Some of his men made from two and a half to three days' work on an individual day. Calculating from the pay-roll the various proportions of skilled and unskilled workmen, and averaging their wages at $3.00 per day for 94 days, we find that 66 men must have been continuously engaged in or about the portion of the 800 feet which was open at any one time. When we add to these the nine carts, carters, and horses, the workmen of the Highway Department, and those of the Water Department, below mentioned. the aggregation must have seriously incommoded itself.

" Horses, carts, and carters form an additional item of $2992.50 in Mr. Charles's charge. They performed 855 days' work in 94 days, and must,

therefore, have mustered nine each day. As most
of the material was stored beside the trench ready
for dumping in, these carts must have served
chiefly by standing and waiting. . . . In addition to all the above, Assistant Commissioner of
Highways S. D. Walter filed a pay-roll amounting to $3410.57 for work done from September 1
to September 30, 1889. It is important to inquire
why a city employé should have had men employed in conjunction with the force of a gentleman
selected to manage the job alone. Mr. Walter's
men seemed to have caught the infection of activ-
ity from Mr. Charles's, as we find here likewise
cases of two and three days' work done by an
individual in a single day.

"Furthermore, the Water Department filed a
pay-roll of $2152.16, and in addition to all these
items we must include Highway Commissioner
George's items, aggregating $12,375.35 for mate-
rials and labor. Wall-paper to the value of $25
was among the materials listed as necessary for
this sewer.

"Scheduling these several bills, we have:

Mr. Allen, Aug. 29 to Sept. 14.	$ 2,444.68
Mr. Charles, Sept. 15 to Dec. 21	31,323.56
Mr. Walter, Sept. 1 to Sept. 30	3,410.57
Water Department	2,152.16
Mr. George, Aug. 29 to Dec. 21	12,375.35
	$51,705.32

Dividing this grand total of $51,705.32 by 800 we
find the cost per foot to be $64.63. It is instruc-

tive to compare with this the cost of $17.50 per
foot for original construction of the sewer on
Twenty-fifth street, identical in all *save being sunk
from 18 to 23 feet deeper*. We have on file the
written opinion of a well-known engineer who
went over the ground shortly after the break.
He ' would have jumped at' a contract to do the
work in three weeks for $10,000, or $12.50 per
foot."

The scientific thoroughness of this report seemed
to leave very little room for discussion. It was
plain as daylight that the city was being plundered of hundreds of thousands of dollars every
year by corrupt combinations of contractors and
officials. Light was thrown, by these disclosures,
upon the eagerness with which seats in the city
council, to which no salary was attached, were
sought by men who could not be suspected of
municipal patriotism, and upon the querulous
complaint of a member from the Fifteenth Ward,
when some question was raised by his fellow-par-
tizans as to his renomination: "It cost me two
hundred dollars to get elected, and I am a poor
man. I think that I am entitled to it for one more
term." Many things in the history of municipal
politics were explained by this report; and as it
was read, dark looks were seen upon many faces,
and ominous mutterings were heard from different
parts of the hall.

When it was finished, the reporters glanced
quickly about, and grasped their pencils to catch

the response of the auditors. Nobody spoke. At length Mr. Strong, the chairman of the committee, slowly rose again.

"I ought to state," he said, "that each of the departments whose work has been reviewed tonight was notified two days ago that such a report would be read at this place and at this time, and the heads of these departments were requested to be present, that any misstatement might be corrected, or any misconception explained. I should be glad to have them called upon at this time."

"Are any of those gentlemen present?" inquired the president.

There was no response.

"The report will be printed in the newspapers of the city," said Mr. Strong, "and I trust that it will be carefully read by every citizen. If any mistakes can be shown, the committee will make haste to rectify them. Our work, let me say, is not yet done. This is the first instalment of our report; we hope to be ready, seven weeks from to-night, with further facts and figures."

THE next week's meeting was devoted to the report of the committee upon the Public Schools, of which the chairman was our friend the parson. This committee had discovered that the schools were, on the whole, in a fair condition of discipline. A vast amount of money had been expended by the city in buildings and apparatus; there were symptoms of jobbery in much of this expenditure, but it had been so carefully covered that the committee were not able as yet to expose it, and therefore they made no reference to it. A more palpable mischief was the operation of one or two companies of school-book publishers, whose relations to certain officers were very suspicious; but this matter was also deferred for further investigation.

"Our schools," said the committee, "are by no means perfect. Certain evils exist which may well be remedied, and of which, after more careful study, we intend to speak. But, on the whole, we are inclined to think that no other interest of the city is more efficiently promoted than that of education. The credit of this is due, mainly, far less to good municipal management than to the character and *esprit de corps* of the class of teachers. There are frivolous and incapable teachers, but there are also not a few high-minded, earnest, unselfish men and women engaged in this calling : the improvements in methods are wholly due to them, the maintenance of moral standards and influences is their work alone.

"The contrast between the teachers, as a class, and the men whom we, as citizens, have selected to supervise their work, is sometimes very painful. Here is a matter of which it is unpleasant to speak, but concerning which silence would be inexcusable. The *personnel* of boards of education in our cities should be carefully studied. Leaving out of sight the composition of the present board, the committee has taken pains to make a list of the names of the men who have held this important trust during the past ten years; it finds that 113 different individuals have been thus employed; that of these two were keepers of livery-stables, one was a huckster, two were cigar-makers, one was the keeper of a newspaper-stand on which the lowest publications are sold, sixteen were saloon-keepers, and twelve were small politicians without any visible means of support. The committee is of the opinion that about half of the members of the Board of Education are usually men of character and cultivation—men who are competent to have an opinion upon educational matters, and fit to associate with the ladies and gentlemen who teach in our schools; but that a considerable percentage of these officers will be found both in morals and manners to be far below the average of the teachers; and that, in intelligence, fully half of them are ridiculously incapable of discharging the duties which they have assumed. The committee has held interviews with all the members of the present Board of Education; it has conversed with them freely; it has sought to draw out their opinions upon educational subjects and methods; it has found among them some very intelligent men: but it does not hesitate to declare that half of these men are conspicuously out of place in such a body. It is amazing that the people will choose

such men for such a service. The truth is, of
course, that the people do not choose them; they
are persons, as a rule, who have some political
ambition, and who hope, by the use of such small
patronage as they can manipulate in connection
with the school-board, to get themselves advanced
to the common council, and finally to the legislature. With such ends in view they secure the
nomination through the use of the party machine. There appears to be no sufficient reason,
in the present order of politics, why men of this
type should not go to the legislature; but we
object to their making the school-board the step-
ping-stone of their ambition. Conceive of putting
a man upon a committee on school-books who
could not intelligently read a page in the majority
of the books submitted to him for examination;
or of making a man a member of the committee
on teachers who could not, to save his life, teach
a single subject in the primary grade. The committee has undertaken to obtain evidence of the
competency of the present school-board which
they will place before the public as fully as they
can. They have requested responses in writing
to a few questions from each member of the present board; they will print copies of these responses, *verbatim et literatim*, in connection with
this report. The names will be suppressed, and
none but the members of the board themselves
shall know who wrote the letters; but the public
will be able to judge, from these responses, of the

intellectual qualifications of the men to whom they have intrusted the work of public education. If the chirography could also be exhibited, the impression, in some cases, would be strengthened. The absurdity of putting educational interests into such hands ought to be obvious. The reply in behalf of some of these illiterate members is that they are capable mechanics, and qualified to give assistance in the work of building. If they could be confined to interests purely physical, this might be well enough; but the fact is that the most difficult and delicate questions respecting books, teachers, methods of instruction, educational policies, are frequently determined, in committee or in the full board, by the casting vote of these men. We have known several such cases. It must be evident that while some knowledge of mechanical construction and of business methods may increase the fitness of a man for this place, yet the first and the indispensable qualification should be some fair degree of education. The selection of men who are utterly illiterate, or who have only the merest smattering of knowledge, to supervise a work so technical and so difficult as that of public education, is such a monstrous blunder that these ignoramuses themselves, if they had the slightest sense of humor, would feel themselves to be unspeakably ridiculous. The committee has prepared, and will place before the meeting, two or three of these letters."

At this point sheets of paper on which portions

of this correspondence had been copied in large
characters were displayed upon the wall in the
rear of the platform. Subjoined are samples:

Rev Morason dear Sir my opinyun is that wimmin shold
not be emploid as principles of scholls exseadin ten rooms
mail principles are mutch better for the larger scholls men
are neaded to manege the older schollars, espeshly the boys.
Yores truly ——

Rev A P Morsen Sir I am not faivorable to the skeem of
replaicing feemales by males as prinsipals of the gramer
scholes for what we can pay we can higher first clas wommin
and secon clas men Id ruther hev a first clas wommman.
Yours respeckfly ——

These letters were greeted with a burst of
amusement, which was soon subdued to a mur-
mur of disgust and cries of " Shame," while many
a flushed and downcast face told of mortification
and annoyance too deep for utterance.

" The committee," concluded the report, " has
only one practical recommendation to make. It
is that every candidate for the school-board be required, before he enters upon his office, to pass the
examination set for pupils of the highest primary
grade, and to furnish a certificate from the school
examiners that he has successfully sustained this
examination. The enactment of a regulation to
the effect should be asked of the legislature. We
trust that this standard will not be thought too
high for the custodians of our public schools, and
we are confident that it would exclude a consider-

able percentage of the men who have held this position in this city within the last two years."

Another burst of laughter greeted the suggestion of the committee, and the meeting dissolved in a buzz of excited and disgusted comment.

VII

In this veracious and painstaking history room cannot be found for all the reports of the Cosmopolis City Club. We have sought to give the reader samples of the method by which its work was done, and of the results secured. The other committees made their reports in regular order, exhibiting careful and conscientious study of the various departments, finding some things to commend, but bringing to light a great deal of slipshod management, and unearthing a vast amount of dubious financiering. The Saturday evening meetings of the club were crowded with interested listeners; it became necessary to seek a larger room for the meetings; and the reports became the talk of the town. Such carefully written and meaty reports were eagerly sought by the newspapers, and were read by thousands who could not attend the meetings; newspapers in other cities began to copy portions of them, and to make comments upon the work of the club.

The utmost pains were taken to make the reports accurate and complete; the president's coun-

sel in his inaugural address was often repeated
and emphasized by him; the determination to
treat every question judicially and scientifically
strengthened as the work proceeded. Several times
alleged errors of fact or inference in the statements made by the committee had been pointed
out by editors or by correspondents; in every such
instance the case was reopened and the evidence
was sifted. Most frequently it was found that the
committee was right; but whenever it was wrong,
the acknowledgment was promptly and generously
made.

It need not be said that the community was profoundly influenced by these publications and discussions. The agitation was bringing forth its
legitimate fruit. On the one hand, reputable
and thoughtful men were profoundly disturbed
and humiliated by the revelations of the club, and
were beginning to manifest an uneasy determination to take matters into their own hands; on the
other hand, the contractors and their allies in the
municipal offices, the purveyors of vice and their
assistants in the police department, were sullen
and truculent; while the managers of the two
political machines were in great doubt as to what
this might lead. The municipal election was ap-
proaching, and the feeling that something must
be done to improve the administration was pretty
general. This was the topic before the executive
committee of the club, assembled in Mr. Tomlinson's private office.

"The pressure is very strong," said Mr. Payne, "for the nomination of a citizens' ticket. Every day I hear men talking about it. They think that no trust can be put in either of the political machines, and that the only hope is in the organization of a new party. Naturally they turn to us to take the lead in this. They say that we have made ourselves masters of the situation; that the people would follow our lead; that now is the time to strike."

"That 's my judgment exactly," responded Mr. Frambes. "I believe that we can redeem this city in the next election. My voice is for war, and I am ready to enlist now."

"Let us see," said Judge Hamlin; "what executive officers do we elect this year?"

"A city clerk," answered Mr. Payne, "an auditor, one member of the fire and police commission, one member of the board of public works, one member of the board of health, and a justice of the peace."

"The mayor is not chosen this year?"

"No; he has one year longer to serve. But he does n't count for much, anyway, under our system. He has no executive authority to speak of."

"How much of a redemption are you going to accomplish, Brother Frambes?" inquired the judge, "if you succeed in electing all these officers upon a citizens' ticket? The real executive power of the city is vested in these boards; you can put one new man into each of them; how much will he be able to effect? It will take three years, at the shortest, to get a majority of your own men into these boards."

"Well, supposing we cannot accomplish everything this year," rejoined the clergyman, "let us start now, and do what we can. We may as well make a beginning. One man in each of these boards may be able to accomplish something."

"That is true," replied the judge, "and we must often be willing to take a small fraction of a loaf rather than go hungry. Yet I doubt whether it is good policy for us to encourage independent nominations this spring. The results would be meager, and I fear the effect upon the popular mind. Things would go on in the old way, in spite of our apparent political success, and the unthinking would be apt to conclude that we had accomplished nothing, and would lose faith in our leadership."

"But you agree, Judge Hamlin," persisted the clergyman, "that nothing substantial will ever be done for the reform of our city government, until city politics are divorced from national politics?"

"Yes; that is clear."

"And that can be done only by the formation of new parties?"

"Certainly; that is the only way."

"Why, then, should we not immediately organize a new party?"

"Because the time is not ripe."

" You mean, I suppose, that we could not elect our ticket. But is it not best to start the organization,—to plant the seed,—and let it germinate and grow? Is n't that the way to form a party?"

" Plant your seed—yes, when you 've got a seed to plant. But there 's the rub. Now, parson, let me ask a question or two. You agree with me, doubtless, in believing that the parties which we form ought to be permanent organizations. The government of cities, like the government of the State and the nation, must be by parties; and these parties must not be mere temporary aggregations of men, but permanent political associations."

" Well, yes; I dare say."

" A party cannot live a healthy life—indeed, has no right to live—unless it stands for something, or has some organic ideas."

" Agreed. Go on."

" Well, then, what will your citizen party, or whatever you call it, stand for in our municipal campaigning? What will be your organic idea?"

" It will be a Law and Order party, I trust. It will stand for the enforcement of the law, and the suppression of vice and crime."

" Do you think that that would be a good and sufficient basis for a municipal party?"

" Yes; the very best. Why not?"

" We are looking forward, remember, to a permanent division of the community. It is necessary to the healthful operation of party govern-

6

ment that the parties be numerically pretty evenly
balanced. Your party would be the Law and Order party. What would the party opposed to you
be?"

"The Lawless and Disorderly party, I suppose," answered the parson, laughing.

"Do you think that it would be a good thing
to have the community permanently and pretty
evenly divided upon that issue—to have about
half of the citizens registered as saints and the
other half as sinners?"

"Well, I should be very glad," parried the
clergyman, "to get half of them creditably registered as saints."

"Doubtless; but would you have two political
parties formed upon this line of division?"

"N-no; perhaps not."

"I should say very decidedly not. I do not
think that it would be a salutary condition. Political discussion between two such parties would
not be edifying. The attempt to perpetuate such
distinctions would be in every way pernicious.
It would make Pharisees of the saints, and fiends
of the sinners. But the proposition is not within
the range of possibilities. You could not, let us
hope, get a moiety of this community to organize
in the support of lawlessness and disorder."

"Well, no; I suppose not. But, then, I see no
reason why the law-abiding citizens should not
combine, and take the administration of the affairs of the city into their hands. They need not

call themselves a Law and Order party; but they would be a Law and Order party just the same."

"That is, you would have them combine for the sake of getting the offices. You would have a party destitute of principles, but animated by certain forms and patriotic sentiments. But such a party as that would very quickly degenerate. No; you cannot organize healthy politics on any such basis. I quite agree with the rest of you in believing that municipal politics must in some way be divorced from national politics, but it must not be divorced from political principles. We must have political organizations in all our cities — organizations based upon ideas, social or economic, which have direct and exclusive reference to the affairs of municipalities. These ideas and principles must be such that there can be honest differences among men concerning them, so that the community can safely sway itself upon opposite sides of them."

"But I don't see," persisted the parson, "how any such division as that can exist. There's a right and a wrong in everything, and I cannot understand how you can get away from that fact in politics. I take it that in every contest one party must be right, and the other party wrong."

"That," replied the judge, "if you will pardon me for saying it, is one of the most mischievous of political errors. The attempt to carry theological, or, perhaps I should say ethical, distinctions into party divisions often creates confusion.

I do not mean to deny that the individual must
be governed by ethical principles in his political
action; but the notion that parties must needs divide on ethical grounds is a great mistake. It is
no more true that there 's a right and a wrong in
every social antagonism than that there is a right
and a wrong in every physical antagonism. The
centripetal and the centrifugal forces in the solar
system are opposed to each other; which is right
and which is wrong? Attraction and repulsion
resist each other in the constitution of matter;
which is right and which is wrong? The harmony of the universe results from the balancing
of antagonistic forces. All healthy political action follows the same law. It is just as necessary
that there should be two parties in every well-
ruled popular government as that the centrifugal
force should be balanced by the centripetal. Each
party stands for a principle which is essential to
the stability and growth of society. The welfare
of the State results from the strenuous and effective advocacy of both these antagonistic principles. The average partizan always thinks that
his party is all right in its aims and that the
other party is all wrong, but this is because the
average partizan is not a philosopher. No healthy
party division has ever been long maintained, or
ever will be, except upon such distinctions as I
have indicated. The two great parties of England have, through all their history, been divided

upon the question of the centralization or the diffusion of political power, and that has been substantially the question between the two parties in American politics. Here is a legitimate issue. For some purposes power must be centralized, and for other purposes it must be diffused. In some emergencies we need a strong government, but it may become too strong. The party which seeks to strengthen it is right, and the party which seeks to limit its power is also right. Now, if it be possible to find, in municipal politics, some such line of division as this, we may be able to organize municipal politics upon a safe and healthy basis. Can you point out any such logical and philosophical division?"

"Not at a moment's notice, judge. But perhaps you can. You have thought the matter over pretty carefully; can you not outline for us the issues on which we may divide in local politics?"

"No; that is equally absurd. Parties are born, not manufactured. They spring from the needs of the hour. They are the outcome and expression of social and economic tendencies which civilization produces. I think that I can see a faint seam in our social structure which is to develop, presently, into such a line of cleavage; but I am not going to risk my reputation as a prophet by pointing it out to-night."

"What, then, would you have us do in the coming campaign? Ought we not to try to utilize for the improvement of our administration the force of public opinion which has been generated in these discussions?"

"By all means. But it seems to me that our best course in this crisis is to act through the existing parties. Doubtless there will be a strong disposition in both of them to put the best foot forward. Let us encourage that. Let us try to get decent candidates nominated by both parties; and when the nominations are made let us exercise our independence in voting for the best without distinction of party. Meantime let us go right on with our work of investigation and discussion, bringing hidden things to light, and subjecting all our municipal machinery and its workings to the most careful scrutiny."

"The thing that discourages me," said Mr. Harper, "is the fact that, do the best we may, we can achieve only a fractional success at the coming election. As Mr. Payne has told us, only one fourth or one fifth of an executive is to be chosen at this time. I fear that the new members of these boards will have but little influence upon their policy, and that things will go on in the old way. It will take at least three years to elect a majority of these governing boards; whether we can keep up the public interest through all this long campaigning I do not know. We have managed to hold the public attention for six months; but unless we are able pretty soon to show some practical gains, I fear that we shall lose our audience."

"That," answered Mr. Payne, "is the precise difficulty. Under the present charter we shall never be able to accomplish very much. The system of government which we are trying to work is one which seems to have been contrived for the dissipation rather than the utilization of the force of public opinion. The first step in the direction of reform is not the organization of new parties, but such a reconstruction of the governmental machinery as shall enable the motive power, which is public opinion, to act directly and effectively toward the ends of government. But that is too big a question to raise to-night. As the chairman of the section upon the workings of the charter, I hope to have something practical to suggest very soon."

The waiting policy suggested by the president was adopted by the club in the municipal campaign. Those who had been prominent in its discussions soon found themselves possessed of considerable political influence. The gentlemen in charge of the political machines of both parties seemed anxious to consult them respecting nominations, and the candidates presented on each side were rather better than the average. In the words of a modern statesman, the machinists had found it expedient "to pander a little to the moral element in the community." The victory in the election was won by the outs, since the public assumed, not very logically, that the abuses exposed were the fault of the party in power. The result of this victory was not, however, perceptible in the administration. The police department did not change its policy; the favored contractors kept their places at the public crib; the reign of inefficiency and rascality was as firm as ever.

The sentiment of the "powers that were" found forcible expression, now and then, at secret conclaves in the city hall.

"I suppose," said Dugan, "that those blatherin' Mugwumps think they 've done us up for good, because they 've got a man of their own on our board in place of old Murphy. Much good that 'll do them! If they had had ordinary common sense they would have let Murphy alone. He was a better man for them than the one they 've got. Fact is, I 'm mighty glad to git shet o' Murphy. He was gittin' too many notions in his head."

"Don't you worry about the new man," rejoined Benson. "He is n't going to make us any trouble. I know how to handle him. He 'll kick, no doubt, for one or two meetings; that 's what he 's paid to do; but I 've got a lasso to use on him. Keep quiet, and see if I don't bring him round."

"Ye can rest aisy in yer minds, gentlemen," said O'Halloran. "This shtorum is mostly wind. It 'll blow over soon. I 've seen too mony of such flurries. These silk-stockinged chaps are up in arrums now and ag'in, but they soon find out that reforrumin' the city is a long and a dirty job, and they drap it as sudden as they tuk it up."

"The only thing that makes me anxious," said Lumley, the contractor, "is a symptom or two that I've noticed of a disposition to reconstruct our charter. If they get to work at that, there's no telling how much mischief they may do. These new-fangled one-man-power governments, like the one they've got over in Oleopolis, are very troublesome things for a business man to deal with — so my friends over there tell me. The only safety for us is in maintaining our present conservative form of government, that cannot be overturned by any sudden movement of popular prejudice. If we had had that kind of a charter, what would have become of us in the last election?"

"Thrue for ye, my boy," answered O'Halloran. "That's the p'int we must be after guardin'. None of yer blanketed municipal despotisms for Cosmopolis! That's the very thing that these Mugwumps 'll be foistin' upon us. We must watch them. Eternal veegilance is the pr-r-rice o' leeberty."

CHAPTER III

WHAT THE CLUB ACCOMPLISHED

VIII

IF Mr. Reginald Payne's committee on Charter Reform could have heard the conversation among the authorities at the city hall, reported in our last chapter, they would have been confirmed in their conviction that the first thing to do was to reorganize the city. With that business in hand the committee is now assembled in Mr. Payne's private office. The other members of the committee are Mr. Graves, a retired lawyer who has given much study to municipal questions, and Mr. Davis, a wealthy banker; the three officers of the society are also present, their wisdom having been sought in this important matter. The meeting is purely informal; it is hoped that talk may help to clear the question of some of its obscurity, and to lead toward some practical plan.

"We might," said Mr. Tomlinson, "get a new charter with no trouble to ourselves, as they did in Vinopolis last winter. The political "outs" of the city had the majority in the legislature; so the managers of the municipal machine proceeded to fabricate a new form of government for the city, took it down to the capital, and rushed it through the legislature, changing the entire system of government, removing all the old officers, and providing for the appointment of the new officials by a local magnate of their own party."

"Perhaps you have n't heard," answered Mr. Payne, "that since the majority of the legislature was changed at the last election, the ejected Vinopolitans are now before that body with a bill simply 'reversing the ripper,' as they call it — pitching the incumbents out of office, and reinstating their own gang. This is a game that the legislatures of several of our States are learning to play; it begins to look as though the reorganization of cities for partizan purposes would soon become a large part of the legislative program."

"They will not try that little game on us," said Judge Hamlin. "It is only when the people are utterly apathetic that any such scheme will be attempted. The people of this city are too wide awake just now to permit such an imposition.

"And yet," answered Mr. Payne, "the legal assumption is that the corporation of a city is the creature of the legislature. May not the legislature do what it will with its own?"

"It is not only a legal assumption," replied Mr. Graves, "it is a constitutional provision. By the constitution of our own State, and of several other States, the legislature has unlimited authority to make, unmake, and remake city charters, and the people of the cities have no power whatever to the contrary."

"That is very true," answered Judge Hamlin. "The legislature has this power. It is, in my judgment, a dangerous power. I hope to see the constitution amended so that the legislature shall have power only to enact a general law, with certain wise limitations, under which all cities must organize. Such a general law is needed, and its provisions and prohibitions should be well studied. But having laid down the general principles on which all local communities should do their business, the legislature should be compelled to take off its hands, and to permit the people to govern themselves. This means that they shall have the power, by conventions which may be held periodically, and for which the general statute shall provide, to frame their own charters; these charters to be submitted to popular vote. The courts of the State could decide whether these charters were in harmony with the general statute. Home rule, to this extent, must be given, as I believe, to American cities."

"But would not this be dangerous business?" inquired Mr. Davis. "Would you dare to give so much power as this to the hordes of foreigners who crowd our cities? Would it not be safer to leave them under the control of the legislature? Is not the morality and intelligence of the State at large rather higher than that of the cities?

Has not the State an interest in having the cities well governed?"

"One question at a time," answered the judge. "The State at large has an interest in good municipal government, but the people of the rural districts are not competent to regulate the business of the cities. Whether the political morality of the country is higher than that of the city, I will not venture to decide; my experience with country members in the legislature is not altogether reassuring. As to the question whether it is not safer to leave the cities under the control of the legislature, there is this to say: we have tried that policy for a good many years, and the result is before us — 'the one conspicuous failure of the United States.' I do not think that our cities could have been in a much worse condition if they had been permitted to govern themselves. It is dangerous, no doubt, to give power to the denizens of our cities. Democracy involves a good deal of risk. I do not pretend to believe that we have yet passed the danger-point in city or nation. I don't know that we shall ever pass it. Jackson was probably nearer right than he knew when he said that the vigilance which guards our liberties must be eternal. Home rule in cities is dangerous, but it is the principle on which our institutions rest, and I, for one, am not going to admit that democracy is a failure until it has been fairly and thoroughly tried. It is the American idea—the Anglo-Saxon idea, indeed — that local communities shall be responsible for their own order and peace. There is no other way, that I know of, by which local patriotism and public spirit can be aroused and kept active. When the business men of any community know that their salvation from anarchy and financial ruin depends wholly upon themselves,— that they cannot call upon the legislature to deliver them from the bandits into whose hands they have suffered themselves to fall, but must either bestir themselves or be plundered,— they are likely to take a more serious view of their responsibilities. Therefore, I hope to see the day when such interventions of the State legislature in local affairs as are now practised in many of our States shall be impossible everywhere. We must prepare and push a constitutional amendment to this effect. But meantime we must make the legislature understand that it must not interfere with our government for party purposes; that we propose, not as partizans, but as citizens, to reshape our own charter; and that they must give us what we ask for. The power is all theirs, but they must exercise it at our behest. I think that it will be possible to make such a demonstration before them that they will be constrained to yield to our demand. If we have n't the form of home rule, we can get the substance of it, if we stand together and fight for it."

"That is what we are here for," said Mr. Payne. "And now we want to consider, I suppose, in a

general way, what form this new charter shall
take; what shall be its leading features — its con-
structive ideas. Any suggestions along that line
are pertinent."

" What do you say," inquired Mr. Davis, " to
the plan of substituting for our present boards of
Police, Public Works, Public Health, and so forth,
non-partizan boards, with an equal representation
of each party on every board ? Would not that
do away with some of the worst evils ? "

" What makes you think so ? " inquired Hathaway.

" Well, it seems that partizanship is the source
of many of our miseries, and this ought to muzzle
the partizans. I know that some of our cities
have non-partizan police boards, and I have heard
that they are working well."

" Possibly," answered the carpenter; " but in
Oleopolis, where I lived for ten years, they tried
it, and it did n't work at all. Everybody said that
the police were more inefficient and corrupt under
that scheme than they had ever been before. Instead of shutting partizanship out, it brought it
in bodily to control the administration. The bill
seemed to recognize the fact that places on the
force were spoils to be distributed among the
heelers, and they were divided accordingly. No
man stood any chance to get a place on the board
unless he was an active political worker in one
party or the other. It is ridiculous to call such
a board " non-partizan "; its main business is the

service of party. You might call it bi-partizan—
that is the proper name for it."

"Mr. Hathaway is quite right," responded
Graves. "I have studied the history of these bi-
partizan boards, and it is, as a rule, precisely
what he has described. An additional weakness
is the failure to fix responsibility. Neither party
is responsible—nobody is responsible—for the
administration. It is far better that the party
in power should have the entire control of the
different departments of the government, and
then the people know whom to punish if there is
inefficiency or corruption. I trust that we shall
have nothing to do with so-called non-partizan
machinery."

"I trust," said Tomlinson, "that we shall have
nothing to do with boards of any kind. I believe that the whole scheme of executive boards
in municipalities is a device of Satan. In nine
cases out of ten the board is the mother of im-
becility, the nurse of irresponsibility, and the
cradle of rascality. I'll have none of them!"

"You are waxing sententious, Tomlinson,"
laughed Payne.

"My mind is clear on this one point, at any
rate," replied the manufacturer. "I have watched
the operation of these boards in this city and elsewhere until I have had good ground for my opinion. Where they are not corrupt, they are miser-
ably inefficient. Partizan or non-partizan, it makes
but little difference; they are all abominations."

"This brings directly before us," said Payne,
"the one important question respecting the
form of our charter. I suppose that we shall
organize our government after the American
plan, with legislative, executive, and judicial departments. There is n't anything absolutely
binding, perhaps, in this threefold division, but
we Americans don't seem to be able to get away
from it. We must provide for one or more police
justices; we must have a legislative council, with
one or two chambers and with certain powers;
but the main question, probably, is the distribu-
tion of executive functions. At present, as Mr.
Tomlinson has reminded us, this power is par-
celed out among certain boards — the Board of
Public Works, which has the care of streets, sewers, markets, and so forth; the Water Commissioners; the Fire and Police Board, which has the
exclusive control of the Fire Department and the
Police Department; the Board of Health, possess-
ing also certain police powers intrusted to it by
the legislature, in which it is independent of all
the other boards; and the Board of Education.
All these boards are elective; most of them are
composed of five members, one of whom is elected
every year to serve five years. Under this arrangement the mayor has almost no power at all.
He is *ex officio* a member of the Police Board; but
the statute gives each of the other four members
exactly the same power that he possesses, and he
is therefore a practical nonentity. Each of these

7

boards is independent of all the others; there is
no consultation among them; they are often at
cross purposes. The Board of Public Works
tears up the pavement one year to put down a
sewer; the next year the Water Commissioners
tear it up again to put down a new main; the
next year the Board of Public Works authorizes
the gas company or the electric light company to
rip it up again for its purposes. The pavements,
for which the people are heavily taxed, are half de-
stroyed by this management, and the streets of the
city are kept in constant disorder. No man who
watches the operations of these boards can be ignorant of the deplorable lack of unity which they
constantly display. Any private business would
be ruined in a year under such a crazy scheme."

"Yes," answers Tomlinson; "and there is no
more unity in them than there is among them.
Each board is apt to be at loggerheads in its own
councils. Take the Police Board. Everybody
knows that the inefficiency of the Police Department is mainly due to the fact that there are five
heads, and that when one is ready to move the
others are not. The mayor is nominally the head
of the department, and issues orders to the men;
but the board can rescind his orders at any meeting. After Harper's scathing exposure of the
complicity of the police with crime, the mayor
was inclined to make an effort to enforce some of
the laws, and he ordered the chief of police to
close up the gambling-places. So the chief went

around and told the gamblers — with his tongue in his cheek, I suppose — that they had better shut up (*sotto voce*, 'for a night or two'), which they accordingly did, but within a week were running again full blast. The newspapers of the opposition soon began to score the mayor because his orders were disobeyed, and he called the chief and wanted to know about it. The chief said that he guessed the gambling-places were shut up; at any rate, that he had ordered them to be, and that he would see about it. But he went his way, like one of those Scripture characters 'who, seeing, see not.' That night I met him at the railway station. O'Kane has always been rather chummy with me, and when I asked him how he was getting on in his fight with the gamblers, he said, 'Oh, that's all quiet. The mayor wants to be good just now, and he's been stirring things up a little; but the fact is, the mayor's only one man, and there are three men on that board who have told me to go slow in this business. You see where I am. My hands are tied.' That is the practical working of most of these boards. They are contrived for the obstruction, not for the despatch, of business. We shall never have efficient government until they are extirpated and swept away, root and branch."

"Yet," said Payne, "I have no doubt that the mayor might get those gambling-places closed if he were determined to do it. He might find ways of getting over those obstructions."

"Yes; I doubt not," replied Tomlinson. "But it is perfectly easy for him to throw the responsibility of his inaction upon the board; and the members of the board are jointly and severally responsible, by the terms of the law — that is to say, nobody is responsible. The system destroys responsibility. No one can be held to account for such a frightful neglect of duty as that which we are now confronting."

"How about that scheme which they are trying in Frumentopolis?" asked Mr. Davis. "There they have abolished the various departmental boards, and have put the whole executive power into the hands of four men, only three of whom can belong to one political party."

"One board is better than six, no doubt," replied Tomlinson, "just as one boil is less painful than half a dozen, but all that I have said about divided responsibility applies to this four-headed executive. Why, in the name of all that is intelligible, do people insist upon applying to municipal government a different standard from that which they apply to all other forms of government? Why should the executive power of a city be given to a board of four men? Are there any political analogies for such a proceeding? Is there any experience which warrants the belief that such a scheme would be practicable?"

"I don't know that there is any experience which bears precisely upon this point," answered Graves; "but there is a good deal of English ex-

perience to show that a large governing body may
govern very well. All English cities are governed
by large councils. The council is simply a committee of the citizens, and its executive work is
divided among subcommittees. The mayor is
chosen by the council, and he is only its presiding
officer ; he has very little executive power."

"That is correct," replied Judge Hamlin; "but
I believe that the committee in charge of each department generally employs a single superintendent, or head clerk, to direct its work, and that
this officer is permanent. The committee does
not interfere with the details of administration."

"In some cases that is true," answered Mr.
Graves. "But it is hard for us to follow English
precedents. England is governed by her Parliament, her executive officers must be members of
Parliament, directly and immediately responsible
to Parliament for every one of their acts. English
municipal government is somewhat analogous to
the national government. Englishmen ought to
be able to make their machinery work; they are
familiar with it. I do not think that we could
do it, and I find that it is already beginning to
be questioned, even among Englishmen, whether
their scheme will not break down in their hands.
I have brought with me a late number of an English quarterly, in which it is freely acknowledged
'that the attempt to govern London by means of
a committee of one hundred and thirty-seven persons is fraught with the gravest possible incon-

venience. The scheme of the Local Government
Act of 1888,' this reviewer goes on, ' is for London
nothing less than administration by public meeting, and it was only by means of the most careful
manipulation that a complete breakdown of the
machinery did not take place during the past three
years. The first County Council for London only
avoided administrative shipwreck by splitting itself into a multitude of subcommittees to which
special duties were assigned, and in moments of
difficulty by placing itself unreservedly in the
hands of such skilful pilots as Lord Rosebery
and Sir John Lubbock.' I have the printed docket
of business for the London County Council for
one day,—July 21, 1891,— with the reports of
committees to be considered on that day, compris-
ing not less than one hundred and twenty distinct
items of business, covering more than forty large
folio pages. It was not expected, of course, that
all this business could be done on that one day;
but the perusal of this docket is sufficient to indicate the enormous complication of interests coming
under the supervision of this body. It is as plain
as the daylight that no individual in that body
could act intelligently upon half of these questions.
The London County Council is a magnificent body
of men, but its abilities are certainly overtaxed.
This seems to be admitted on all hands. The need
of an entirely new organization of its business is
manifest. And this reviewer says : ' For ourselves,
we have no doubt that what London needs is, as

has been pointed out by Sir John Lubbock and
Lord Rosebery, *a responsible executive*. To secure
this, the County Council must begin by treating
itself not as a directly administrative body, but as
a local assembly of one hundred and thirty-seven
" select" men — chosen to appoint and supervise
the actual administration of the metropolis.   The
council's first business should be to elect from
among themselves a chairman, to act as a sort of
prime minister; their next, to select, on his advice,
fifteen or sixteen councillors to act with him as
heads of the various departments of work undertaken by the council. These heads of departments
and the chairman could constitute a sort of met-
ropolitan cabinet, and would form the executive
of London.'   The choice of the heads of the executive departments by the city council is, perhaps, a scheme worth considering, though it is
probable that the American plan of choosing
executives by popular vote would work better with
us.   But the main idea which these critics of the
London system are trying to realize is the definition of responsibility.   'It is one of the chief
safe-guards of the Constitution,' says this writer,
'that a minister must be found to take the complete responsibility for every act done in the name
of the sovereign, in order that, if that act is ill
advised, the country may know on which instru-
ment of state to impose its censure. The sovereign
can do no wrong and bear no blame; therefore,
before he acts, some person must be found ready

to accept any blame that may attach to what is done in the sovereign's name. In the same way, though for a different reason, it is impossible to attach blame to a board or a council. If we are wise, then, we shall insist that no act shall be done in the name of a board or a council so important as the London County Council, for which some definite person is not willing to take the responsibility.' I believe that this principle of concentrating and fixing responsibility is just as sound in America as in England; that it lies at the very foundation of representative government."

"Can any man explain," demanded Tomlinson, "why this sound principle is constantly set at naught in our municipal machinery? Why is it that the people of our cities will not see that they cannot have efficient administration until they wisely subdivide their business, and make some individual responsible for every department of it? Why is it that they are bound to believe that a monster with five heads, five pairs of eyes, five pairs of hands, is more likely to see clearly, judge wisely, and act promptly than a man with one brain, one judgment, and one will?"

"Perhaps," said Davis, "it comes from the democratic notion that in a multitude of councilors there is safety."

"But that," said Tomlinson, "is not the same as saying that in a multitude of bosses there is efficiency."

" Perhaps," said Judge Hamlin, " it is the off-spring of the American tendency to multiply official positions, so that every man may have a public office."

" I am rather inclined to believe," said Hatha-way, " that there is a pretty large class of persons in our cities who have an interest in keeping municipal government inefficient and corrupt, and I think that this arrangement suits them very well."

" Underneath it all," said Payne, " is a profound distrust of the democratic principle. This system of boards and commissions has sprung — as you will find, if you study its origin — from a fear of the people; from an uneasy apprehension that if they are permitted to express their will directly in public matters, they may do a great deal of mischief. Arrangements are therefore made whereby no very decisive changes can be effected in any election. If you have an executive board of five, whose members can be removed only one at a time, it takes the people three years at least to change the character of the board by annual elections. It is almost impossible to keep the attention of the people fixed upon such a matter for three years, and the consequence is that the people's will is practically nullified."

" There is also," said Judge Hamlin, " a dim notion that the main function of city officials is to do mischief, and that the policy should therefore be to give them as little power as possible. The less power they have, the less evil they can do. Municipal governments are adjusted to this estimate of official conduct. It is supposed that by dividing up and parceling out the power the danger will be lessened. A board of five men will act less efficiently than a single man, and is therefore less to be feared. Pessimism of this sort underlies a good deal of our municipal structure. But the trouble is that when we take away the power of these officials to do evil, we also deprive them of the power to do good. We tie their hands so effectually that they can do nothing for us. It is high time that we had learned that popular government rests not on a basis of distrust, but on a basis of confidence ; if we cannot find men whom we can trust, our democracy may as well go into liquidation at once."

"We seem," said Payne, "to be pretty well agreed as to principles. And now let me read the outline of my scheme for a reconstructed charter. It provides for — I. A council of one chamber with legislative functions clearly prescribed. II. Two police justices, to be appointed by the mayor, their terms of office not to be less than five years. III. An executive department, the head of which is the mayor, who is elected by the people to serve for two years. The mayor's executive staff to be composed of (1) a superintendent of police ; (2) a chief of the fire department ; (3) a water commissioner ; (4) a superintendent of streets and sewers ; (5) a health officer ; (6) a city solicitor, or legal adviser of the administration.

All these officers of the mayor's cabinet to be appointed by the mayor himself, without confirmation, and to be directly responsible to him, and removable at his pleasure. Their terms of office should expire with his own. The mayor to hold weekly conferences with the members of his staff, requiring each of them to report directly to him the transactions of his department. In addition to these officers of the mayor's staff, a city clerk, a city auditor, and a city treasurer are to be elected by the people, each for the term of two years — not when the mayor is chosen, but in alternate years. As to the Board of Education, I am not clear. My own decided conviction is that it should be appointed by the mayor; that it should consist of not more than nine men; that three of these should be appointed each year to serve for three years, and that they should not represent districts or wards, but should be the best men obtainable in the city. Whether a measure as radical as this could be carried at present, I doubt; and I would not endanger the plan by an unpopular feature. About all the rest my mind is pretty well made up. This scheme gives us, for substance, what we want—a single executive, with a clear definition of responsibility."

"The subordinates in your six departments — who would appoint them?" inquired Davis.

"The head of each department," answered Payne; "except that I mean to provide for a civil-service commission which shall certify to the Police and Fire Departments, and to the city auditor and city treasurer, candidates from among whom their appointments must be made."

"Would n't it be better," asked Davis again, "to give the council the power of confirmation in the cases of heads of departments, and perhaps of some other offices? That is in accordance with our national constitution."

"Yes; and that is one of the most questionable features of our national constitution," answered Payne. "No harm has resulted from it, so far as cabinet officers are concerned, because it is an unwritten law that these officers shall always be confirmed without questioning. No intelligent man would ever undertake the responsibilities of the Presidency if he could not name the heads of departments without dictation from anybody. In the case of some other offices, the Senate sometimes exercises its veto power; but it is an open question whether more harm than good has not resulted from this extension of its prerogative. So far, however, as the immediate advisers of the President are concerned, his power to select them is practically absolute. The constitutional provision to the contrary is abortive, and it would be senseless for us to copy that."

"Your scheme," suggested Graves, "is substantially the same as that which is in operation in Kirkopolis and Agapopolis."

"Yes; substantially. The principle which they have embodied in their charters is the one that I am after. The details may be varied, but the thing to aim at is a single executive, chosen by the people and directly responsible to them."

"The millennium has n't come yet to Kirkopolis or Agapopolis," answered Davis. "I have noticed in their newspapers that even under the reformed charters peculation is charged against officials, and many dubious deeds are done."

"Of course," answered Payne. "There will be carelessness and rascality under the best system that can be devised. We are not going to have the millennium in Cosmopolis, reform we our charter never so wisely. But there has been great improvement in both those cities, as every intelligent man testifies; and nobody there wants to go back to the old system. We can have the same measure of improvement here, and even greater, if we will work for it."

"Well," said Judge Hamlin, rising, "you have the general idea. Work it out carefully. Get all the light you can from the experience of other cities. Frame your charter in simple, untechnical language; submit it to the club for their approval; and when it is perfected we will refer it to a mass-meeting of the citizens."

IX

It was a field night at the city hall when the Cosmopolis City Club presented its plan for a reorganization of the city government. The charter which Mr. Payne's committee had worked out was as simple and concise in its expression as they could make it; it had been printed in full in all the newspapers, and had been under discussion for more than a week, and the utmost pains had been taken to enlighten the public respecting the organic law which the legislature was to be asked to enact for the government of the city. The members of the club had not been idle. They had personally invited large numbers of the intelligent citizens to be present at the mass-meeting; they had determined that the best elements of the population should be represented, and the hall was filled at an early hour. The mayor was in the chair, and Mr. Payne opened the discussion by reading and briefly explaining the sections of the charter.

It was well known to the club that their scheme would be opposed: some of the newspapers had assailed it, and various elements in the community were bent on defeating it. As a matter of course all the corrupt politicians, the contractors, and the lawless classes generally, were in the opposition. The committee strongly hoped that they would reveal their sentiments by open antagonism; but they had evidently held a council of war, and were determined to fight in ambush, putting forward certain puzzle-headed respectabilities to do the talking for them. The main line of opposition was the charge that the proposed system was autocratic and un-American; that it robbed the people of their liberties. It was a one-man power —that was the phrase which was harped upon continually, in the rooms of the ward committees, in the bar-rooms, in the opposition newspapers. Those who, for personal and unworthy reasons, were resisting the reform were shrewd enough to know that this was the most effective weapon they could use. A great many well-meaning but unthinking persons were frightened by the phrase "one-man power," and were made to believe that this plan really threatened to impose upon them some kind of despotism. It was evidently hoped that in this popular meeting this particular gong could be beaten with telling effect. Accordingly, after Mr. Payne had finished his exposition of the charter, and before a word could be said in its favor, a shrewd lawyer of the city, Johnson by name, gained the floor, and was called to the platform. Johnson was a man of decent appearance, of some literary pretensions, and of fluent speech. He was not believed to have any selfish reasons for opposing the charter, but his mind was full of certain hazy political theories with which this scheme of government was not in harmony.

"It is evident," said Mr. Johnson, "that some measure of reform is needed in our municipal government, and the thanks of this community are due to the gentlemen who for so many months have been studying the municipal problem with the purpose of giving us a better government."

The applause at this point was so hearty and so long sustained that Mr. Johnson was somewhat embarrassed.

"Nevertheless," he persevered, "we must be cautious in making changes. Better to bear the ills we have than fly to worse conditions. And I must own that the plan which these gentlemen have submitted strikes me unfavorably. I do not like the idea of putting so much power into the hands of one man. I do not relish the anticipation of living under a dictator. I know it is sometimes said that when our democracy breaks down we shall rush to the other extreme, and call in a despot to rule us; but I hope that we have n't yet come to that. Just think of the enormous amount of patronage that we intrust to the mayor under this scheme! Is there any man here, who knows anything about politics, who cannot see whereunto this will tend? The selfish man who gets this power in his hands will use it, of course, for his own aggrandizement. He can reëlect himself as mayor just as often as he pleases; he can nominate himself to any office that he covets; he can control the nomination of all your legislators, congressmen, judges. It is too much power, I think, to give to one man. We know what kind of men are in city politics, and we know what they are apt to do with such power as this when they get hold of it. I counsel my fellow-citizens to beware how they intrust such enormous political power to one man."

Mr. Johnson's speech was greeted with vigorous cheers from the opposition; but before he had descended from the platform Judge Hamlin arose, and courteously asked him to pause a few moments before returning to his seat.

"Mr. Johnson's objections," said the judge, "are entitled to consideration. Now is the time to consider them. He has stated them briefly, clearly, and forcibly. He is an intelligent and honorable opponent of our plan. I wish, therefore, to beg of him, if his honor the presiding officer will wink at the irregularity, to remain here on the platform for a few minutes, that there may be a little direct conversation between us on the subject. I will ask him a few questions, and he may ask me as many as he chooses. Very likely I shall be obliged to confess my ignorance more than once: that should be no discredit to either of us; the subject is large, and there are aspects of it that neither of us has considered. But I am convinced that we can get at the truth by such a conversation more expeditiously than by set speeches; and if your honor please, and if the meeting consent, I should like to try that method."

The hearty cheers of the assemblage gave full indorsement to the proposition of the judge.

"Well, then," said Judge Hamlin, "Mr. Johnson assumes that the city patronage is likely to be dispensed by the mayor for his own interests. It is now dispensed by about forty different officials.

I suppose that we must therefore assume that the forty are making the same use of it."

"That may be granted," answered the lawyer.

"Is it reasonable to say that forty selfish politicians, scrambling after the city patronage that they may use it for their own aggrandizement, will inflict less injury upon the community than one man who uses it in the same way? Are forty small bloodsuckers to be preferred to one big bloodsucker?"

The audience laughed and cheered, and Mr. Johnson was saved the trouble of answering the question.

"Each of these forty," said Judge Hamlin, "has his own followers, for whom, on this supposition, he is trying to find places. Suppose that he secures for one of these followers, who is utterly incompetent and unworthy, a place on the police force or in the Fire Department; is the public able in any way to hold him responsible for this bad appointment? Does the public know anything about it."

"Probably not," answered Mr. Johnson.

"It is possible, then, for these forty to fill all the public places with dead-beats and bummers, without the public being able to call anybody to account for the outrage?"

"Doubtless," assented the lawyer.

"To what extent is this done?"

"To a very considerable extent, undoubtedly. Yet there are a great many very good men now in the service of the city."

"Of course; but that is because the forty are not all thieves, because some of them act with public interests in view. I should hope that we might very often find a mayor who would act upon that principle. I am only speaking upon the assumption that politicians always use patronage selfishly. On that presumption the present scheme does not seem to be ideal. But suppose that one of these forty should wish to promote the public interest, rather than his own welfare. Take a man on the police commission, or the street commission, who wants to improve the service. How much can he accomplish, standing alone?"

"Not much."

"Suppose that by dint of courage and perseverance he should succeed in removing some abuses, and in purifying the administration. How much credit would he get for it?"

"Very little."

"So that, as things are now arranged, it is almost impossible for any man, by faithful performance of his public duty, to gain any good reputation for himself?"

"It is much as you say."

"Our present system assumes that every official will be selfish and dishonest, and gives him a great many chances to be selfish and dishonest; it assumes that nobody will act purely and honorably, or wish to receive any praise for so acting. Do you think that we have any right to look for good administration under such a system?"

"It seems that we are not finding it, at any rate."

"You spoke of the power that the mayor would have under our system to promote his own fortunes by the use of the city patronage. Whatever he did in this direction would have to be done, would it not, in plain sight of all the people? He would have the entire responsibility for all his appointments; the people would have their eyes all the while fixed on him, and would be able to judge of the motives for which they were made."

Mr. Johnson assented.

"Do you think that the executive who uses patronage in this way, in full view of the people, is morally certain to aggrandize himself in the process? Have you ever heard of anybody who failed in such an undertaking?"

The hit was palpable, and the audience burst into a roar of laughter, which broke out again and again. Mr. Johnson had been rather conspicuously allied with a noted machine politician of the State who had only recently met with ignominious defeat in this very enterprise. The lawyer made the best of his discomfiture by joining in the laugh.

"I don't think," he said, when the tumult subsided, "that a man infallibly succeeds by the use of patronage; but I think that, as a rule, it gives him an enormous advantage."

"On the contrary," replied the judge, "I believe that our political history will show that it is an enormous disadvantage to any man to have such patronage, and to use it selfishly. When the responsibility for the use of it can be clearly located, the people are pretty sure to punish condignly the man who uses power for his own aggrandizement. The motive for using this power wisely and patriotically would, I contend, be a thousand times stronger under the system we propose than it is under the present system. But Mr. Johnson referred, also, to the danger of committing so much executive power to one man. The idea seems to be that the people divest themselves of their liberty, and place themselves in chains, when they intrust to one man so much executive power. It appears to some of our friends that they will no longer be living under a republic, but under a monarchy, if our plan is adopted. But all will admit that under the old system, as well as under the new, the people intrust the executive power to officials; that they temporarily put it out of their hands. Let me ask Mr. Johnson *if it is not as effectually out of the people's control when it is in the hands of forty men as it is when it is in the hands of one man."*

"Doubtless."

"Under the plan we propose, the people loan the executive power for two years to one man, holding him responsible for the right use of it. If it is not properly used, they know exactly whom to blame. At the end of the two years this man must return the executive power directly to the hands of the people. They get it all back again,

every shred of it. If it has been abused, they may
put it into other hands. If it has been wisely
used, they may return it, if they choose, to the
man who has been holding it. Every two years
he must settle his account with them, and restore
to them the power which they had intrusted to
him. That is our plan. Under the scheme which
this city has been trying to operate, the executive
power is all put out of the people's hands into the
hands of forty officials, members of various boards
and commissions. When will the people get it
back again ? "

"It comes back by instalments," answered the
lawyer.

"Yes; it comes back in driblets, in such a way
that it is morally impossible for the people to
replace it wisely. In the first place, nobody can be
very sure whether the driblet that returns this
year has been well used or ill used ; in the second
place, it is only an infinitesimal fragment of
power, anyway, and it seems to make but little
difference to whom it is committed. It is utterly
impossible for the people in any election to make
a thorough improvement in their government, and
naturally they do not care to try. Their hands
are so tied by the red tape of our complicated
executive that they take very little interest in
municipal elections. Now I wish to ask every
man of common sense who listens to me, Which
of these plans gives the greater power to the
people ? Under which of them can the people

bring their power more directly and more effectively to bear upon the administration? Under which of them would the people have the clearer consciousness of their power, the deeper sense of their responsibility? I affirm, and I challenge any intelligent man in this audience to dispute the affirmation, that the system of government by a manifold series of boards and commissions reduces the popular power to a minimum, while the system which we propose, of a single responsible executive, exalts, magnifies, and confirms popular power. Your system rests upon distrust of the people; our system rests upon faith in the people. That is the radical difference between them. I call upon my friend here on the platform to dispute this statement if he can."

"I am not now prepared to argue the point," said Mr. Johnson.

"I call upon any opponent of our plan in this house," resumed the judge, "to stand up and deny my affirmation if it is not true. No man answers. Let us have done, then, with this nonsense about the 'one-man power.' Every man who uses this phrase to stigmatize our charter means to convey the notion that its aims are aristocratic, or autocratic, rather than democratic. I suppose that some have ignorantly imagined that this might be true. No intelligent man will make any such suggestion unless he is a demagogue. A very intelligent business man put the matter in a nutshell, the other day, when he said to me, ' What these people call the one-man power is simply the crown of popular sovereignty.' It is that crown, fellow-citizens, which we are trying to place upon your heads. We want you to govern this city, and to see and know that you are governing it. We want to enable you to honor and reward those who serve you faithfully, and to depose and punish those who are false to your interests. We claim for our charter that it restores to the people the power of which they have long been robbed."

The ringing cheer with which these last sentences of Judge Hamlin were greeted showed that the victory of the charter was won already. Mr. Johnson waited until the applause had subsided, and then quietly said : " If his honor the judge will permit, I think I will return to my seat. I believe that I should enjoy his eloquence rather more if I were permitted to share it with the rest of the audience."

" Very good," answered the judge, laughing with the rest, and extending his hand to the lawyer. " I am greatly obliged to my friend for submitting to my catechism. And I will try to be just as patient and courteous as he has been if he will subject me to the same ordeal."

" No," answered the lawyer; " I will waive the cross-examination."

" Then," continued the judge, " I will take only time to make one more remark. It is objected to our plan that it puts too much power into one man's hands. May I ask whether the power intrusted to our mayor is any greater than that which by the Constitution of the United States is vested in the national executive? All the enormous power of the Federal government, the administration of the civil offices, the control of the army and navy, is committed to one man. The appointment of his cabinet is left to him; all vacancies in the national judiciary, and innumerable other offices, must be filled by him; he is the one man responsible for the executive department of this whole nation. I should like to ask any gentleman present whether he does not think that it is safer and wiser to commit this power to one man than it would be to give it to a triumvirate, or to a commission of five, with equal powers. Does not the single executive give us a purer and a more efficient administration than any such board would give us? Has any man yet been heard of who would dream of applying the complicated method by which our city is ruled to the government of the nation? Does any one suppose that it would be an improvement to replace the single responsible head of the Treasury Department or of the Interior Department by a commission of five men, one to be elected by the people every year to serve for five years? The preposterousness of such a system when applied to the vast affairs of the nation is obvious enough. Why is it not even more preposterous when applied to the smaller affairs of a city? If one man can administer the great concerns of the nation more efficiently than three men; if one man can conduct the enormous business of one of the national departments better than five men, why is it not probable that one man would manage the executive business of our city, or of any one of its departments, more successfully than three men or five men? The fact is, that while, for counsel, it is sometimes wise to enlist a plurality of judgments, for all executive work the principle of a single responsible head is almost uniformly recognized as the only sound principle. The reluctance to adopt it in municipal affairs is a phenomenon which needs explaining. I trust, however, that we are nearly ready to adopt it in this city, and unless I am greatly at fault, this representative assembly of our citizens is prepared to say so with no uncertain sound."

Judge Hamlin was cheered to the echo when he took his seat, and there were cries for Tomlinson.

"My speech will be very short," said the manufacturer, rising. "I wish to reply to one objection which I have heard since I entered the hall. 'It is n't better laws that we want,' said the objector, 'but better men to administer them.' I tell you we want both. This is very delicate and difficult business that we give our city officials to do, and we must have the most skilful workmen we can get, and the best tools, too. The machinery of government must be the best that we can find. Don't tell me that it makes no differeuce what kind of machinery you have; that all that is wanted is good and faithful workmen. The best workmen in this land could not do the work that is now done every day in my factory if they were compelled to work with the tools my men were working with five years ago. So it is with municipal machinery. There are some kinds with which it is difficult to do anything; there are some kinds with which it is much easier to do good work; and we are bound to give the men whom we employ the best possible facilities. Of course the need of employing the best men will not be superseded by any sort of machinery, and the people will always be required to exercise their patriotism in selecting the men to conduct the government under the new charter."

Calls for Hathaway followed the conclusion of Mr. Tomlinson's speech.

"I want to add one word," said the carpenter, "to the speech that has just been made. With better machinery you are pretty sure to get better men. If you give an official a chance to win some credit for his work, you will attract to the service of the city men of honorable ambition. If you give him a chance to serve the public efficiently, you will call into office men of public spirit. Why should any clean-handed, honorable man take a place in our municipal service to-day? He can do nothing, honorably, for himself, and nothing for the city. Under the plan which we propose a man may make a record for himself; and if he has any force in him, he may greatly promote the public welfare. I believe that our plan will result here, as it has resulted elsewhere, in pushing better men to the front, and in sending the bummers to the rear."

Hathaway's speech closed the discussion. When he had concluded the house resounded with cries of "Question," and the resolution indorsing the new charter, and calling on the mayor to appoint a committee of fifty men—an equal number from each political party—to present the matter to the legislature on the following week, and to secure immediate action, went through in a storm of enthusiasm. The noes, indeed, were so few and feeble that the audience greeted their protest with an outburst of good-natured laughter.

X

THE committee of fifty found little trouble in securing from the legislature favorable action upon the charter. Delegations from the classes opposed were present at the capital, and some secret work was done with various members of the legislative committee on municipal affairs; but the representation of the best citizens was so strong, and the popular demand for the charter was a fact so notorious, that the opponents of the scheme made little headway. The bill was rapidly pushed to its third reading, and the new charter went into effect in ample time for the spring election.

Hathaway's prediction that the new measures would call to the front a better class of men was abundantly fulfilled. For many years the office of mayor had gone begging among the better class of citizens. Whenever there had been a spasm of popular virtue, and a determination to secure good government, the laudable purpose had been defeated by the flat refusal of men of character to accept the nomination. "Why," said these gentlemen, "should we soil our hands with the dirty business? The mayor is only a figure-head. You have stripped him of power. What can he do to improve the administration? He can gain no reputation; he can accomplish no reform. We have no time to spend upon such a bootless function."

But now it was clear that the conditions were greatly changed. There was a chance for a man of brains and force to make a record for himself. Men of honorable ambition were not loath to consider the call of their fellow-citizens to this honorable and responsible office. Moreover, it was instinctively felt, even by the party managers, that it would never do to nominate a man for this position whose character was not a guaranty of honest administration. The interests were too important. They knew that if one candidate was more upright and more capable than the other, the mass of the conservative vote of the tax-paying and law-abiding citizens would go directly to that candidate. Party lines had been so weakened by the work of the City Club that the reputable classes would be pretty sure to vote for the most reputable man. The only safety for the party managers lay in selecting the best possible candidate. Hitherto the managers had asked who could carry the saloons and the slums. This year the question was who could carry the tax-paying wards. Accordingly the candidates on both tickets were men of good character. It was freely acknowledged on all sides that the interests of the city would be safe, no matter which party might triumph. Another obvious gain was the lessening of the number of places on the ticket. As a rule, there could be no more than four or five persons to be voted for in each municipal election. It was possible, therefore, for the conscientious voter to inform himself respecting the character of each of the candidates presented to him.

"This simplifies things," said Tomlinson to Payne, one day, as they were looking over the list of nominations printed at the head of the editorial columns in one of the party organs. "I trust that the people will be able to know, this time, for whom they are voting. For myself, I must admit that, in an experience of twenty years, I have never yet voted intelligently in a city election. I always try to inform myself respecting the record and qualifications of every candidate on both tickets; I have never yet succeeded. A good share of my voting has been done in the dark. When the number of candidates is as large as it has been in our elections, very few men, I believe, vote intelligently. Most of us take the goods the gods of the caucus provide for us, and are compelled to be satisfied. Henceforth, with due diligence, a man may be instructed before he votes."

"Yes," answered Payne; "the popular sovereign is more likely, under this plan, to rule with wisdom. The task we have been imposing upon him was quite too difficult. We have bidden him, every year, to pick out twenty or thirty men from among his fellow-citizens to whom he would intrust the responsibilities of government. That overtaxes his intelligence. But when we tell him to pick out three or four men, the chances are that he will make fewer blunders."

It was the evening after the municipal election, and the five directors of the Cosmopolis Public Library had assembled for their weekly meeting. The business was not urgent, and their minds were too full of the events of the day to give much heed to the librarian's report. Payne had picked up Judge Hamlin in the street, and had brought him in, and Harper had similarly introduced Mr. Graves.

"Well, Judge," said Harper, as they seated themselves around the fireplace, "your party is entitled to congratulations. You have the chance of demonstrating to the city the excellence of the new charter. I would rather it had been my party. I 'm quite sure that we would have made a little better job of it ; but you have put it into good hands, and I have no doubt that we shall see a great improvement over past administrations."

" Let us hope so," responded the judge. " If we do not, we shall go out with a whirl, two years from now ; that 's certain."

" One thing is to be noted with sincere rejoicing," said Mr. Graves. " The vote is the heaviest ever polled in a municipal election. The voters were all out ; and it was intelligent interest that brought them out. I am told that much less money has been expended this year than ever before. Men like Spring and Chapman will not spend money to elect themselves. They held a conference about it as soon as they were nominated, and pledged themselves to each other that they would not do it."

" Yes," answered Judge Hamlin ; " it is all very cheering. We are sure to have a great deal better government than we have had for a long time. We are on the right track. We have got the right sort of machinery. Our system rests now upon the true democratic optimism,—the belief that the people can be trusted,— and not upon the pessimistic notion that they must be pushed as far as possible from the thrones of power, and fenced off, by all manner of complicated checks and restraints, from direct participation in the government. I hope that we shall see our laws enforced now as they have not been for many a day. Chapman would n't dare to put a man into that superintendency who has n't the nerve to enforce them. I hope that we shall see the army of contractors put to rout, and a great improvement in the condition of our streets, and a great reduction in the expenses of every department of the government. But we must not be too sanguine. We have made an important gain, but we have n't solved the municipal problem yet."

"What is lacking?" asked Payne.

"The one thing needful is lacking," replied the judge; "that is, a foundation of principles on which municipal politics can be built. I have said this before, but the experience of this election has made it clearer. What have we been contending for in this election? It was simply a question which was the better ticket. The issue with the political managers was of course the spoils of office; with the rest of us it was a choice of administrators. There was no room for intelligent discussion. The campaign has not been in the slightest degree educational. I do not think this good politics. I am sure that it will tend to corruption. The practical interest of the spoilsmen will overshadow the interest which the rest of us will strive to maintain in the selection of good candidates. So long as our municipal affairs remain in the hands of the two national par-

9

ties, our municipal elections will strongly tend to become mere make-weights in State and national politics. It is the best we can do now, but municipal politics will never be clean and healthy until we have municipal issues and municipal parties distinct from those of the State and the nation."

" Where are these issues to come from?" demanded Morison.

" I am not sure; but it seems to me that I see them looming upon the horizon," answered the judge. " Have you observed the fight that the people in Oleopolis have been waging against their gas company?"

" Yes," said Harper; " and the people have won the fight. They have forced the price of gas down to eighty cents a thousand feet, and have compelled the company to pay a heavy annual tribute for its franchise."

" So I read. And have you noticed the sharp questions that the newspapers are beginning to raise respecting the street-railway franchises and the electric-light franchises? It seems to me that the question of municipal ownership of all these natural monopolies is rushing to the front; that it will be upon us in a very few years. For my own part, I believe that these properties must belong to the municipality; that whatever is a practical monopoly the people themselves must own and control. That our cities will soon advance in this direction is evident to me. I trust that there

will be no spoliation of those who have invested
their money in such properties; that they will be
purchased by the cities at a fair valuation. What
to do about the franchises that have been stolen
is a more puzzling question. Our courts of
equity will be taxed to unravel that snarl; let us
trust that we shall not be weak enough to wait
for the revolutionist with his sword to cut it.
But the cities will get possession of the natural
monopolies; of that I feel confident."

"But that," answered Tomlinson, "is the road
to Socialism."

"Yes; that's the road. And we are going in
that direction—no doubt about it. We shall stop
before we get there, I think—a long way short of
a complete collectivism, I believe; but we shall go
that way. Our cities will municipalize certain
important industries. That will be the beginning. Then there will be a strong tendency to
extend this movement. It will be extended. The
city will not only furnish schools, and parks, and
public gardens, and art-galleries; it will find a
number of other things to do for the promotion
of the public welfare, which can be done far more
cheaply and effectively by the coöperation of the
whole people, through their government, than by
private enterprise. And yet there will be vast
realms of industry with which, as I believe, the
municipalities cannot wisely meddle. Individual
initiative and private enterprise will still have a
large part of the world to themselves, and must

be confirmed in their possession of it. And here, as it seems to me, must appear the line of division in municipal politics. It will always be an open question, and a fair question, how far this municipalization of industries shall go, and where it shall stop. Honest men, patriotic men, will differ about this question. You and I, Tomlinson, would differ about it. You are more of an Individualist than I am; I am more of a Socialist than you are. Men of my way of thinking, who see large possibilities in the way of social coöperation through the State for economic ends, will have to be restrained by men of your way of thinking, to whom the liberty of the individual seems the chief good at which legislation should aim. Social progress is to be the result of a wise coördination of these two tendencies. Therefore I expect to see municipal politics based, before long, on this division. There will be a party that tends in the direction of Socialism, and a party that tends in the direction of *laissez-faire;* each party will have a great deal to say for itself; the safety of the community will be in keeping the balance between them."

"Is n't that," said Graves, "substantially the division between the two parties now represented in the London County Council?"

"So I understand," answered Judge Hamlin. "The Progressives are Socialists; their program involves a vigorous interference by the municipality with various industries, and an extension of the powers of government in several directions. They propose to 'take over' the tramways, the street lighting, the water supply, and other monopolies; they intend to adopt a drastic policy in clearing out the slums, in supervising tenement-houses, and in regulating places of amusement; they are carrying what some people call 'paternalism' to lengths which a few years ago would have seemed revolutionary. The Moderates are Individualists; they hold to the old notion that that State is best governed which is least governed; they resist the socialistic tendency. The Progressives are to-day the popular party; but they are very likely to overdo the business, and then the reaction will come, and the Moderates will return to power. But it seems to me that we see in London to-day the logical division between municipal parties—a division which has naturally emerged in the economic and social evolution, and which will just as surely emerge in our own cities, because the conditions are substantially the same. I shall be glad to see the lines drawn in the same way in Cosmopolis and in every American city. Then our municipal politics will have some significance; we shall have parties that stand for something; we shall have policies to advocate, and measures to fight for; our discussions will have direct and practical reference to municipal affairs; and our campaigns will not be a brainless scramble for the spoils of office."

"What will become of the old parties under this arrangement?" demanded Payne.

"They will confine their attention to their own business," replied the judge. "They will manage the State and the national campaigns, and let city politics alone."

"Do you not think that if this were the case, municipal politics would be apt to overshadow national politics?" asked Hathaway.

"In the cities, yes."

"But is it not quite possible that the issues thus raised in the cities would become national?" persisted the carpenter. "Is not the nationalization of certain industries — railroads, telegraphs, telephones, mines, and so forth (those which, according to your own definition, are natural monopolies) — quite likely to be the burning question before many years? Is not this question of the extent to which industries can be profitably nationalized the one which this country has got to face pretty soon? Do we not find in the nation as well as in the city the necessity of drawing the line between State action and private enterprise? Might we not have two national parties, divided by this line, whose discussions and contests would have tenfold more significance than those of the existing political parties? And is it not possible that the municipal parties whose advent Judge Hamlin predicts will gradually become national parties, swallowing up 'the ancient forms of party strife,' and leading in the issues of a new political dispensation?"

" It is not only possible, my friend," replied the judge, rising and taking the carpenter by the hand, "it is in every way desirable. I hope that you and I will both live long enough to see your prophecy fulfilled."